THE ART OF CRAFT

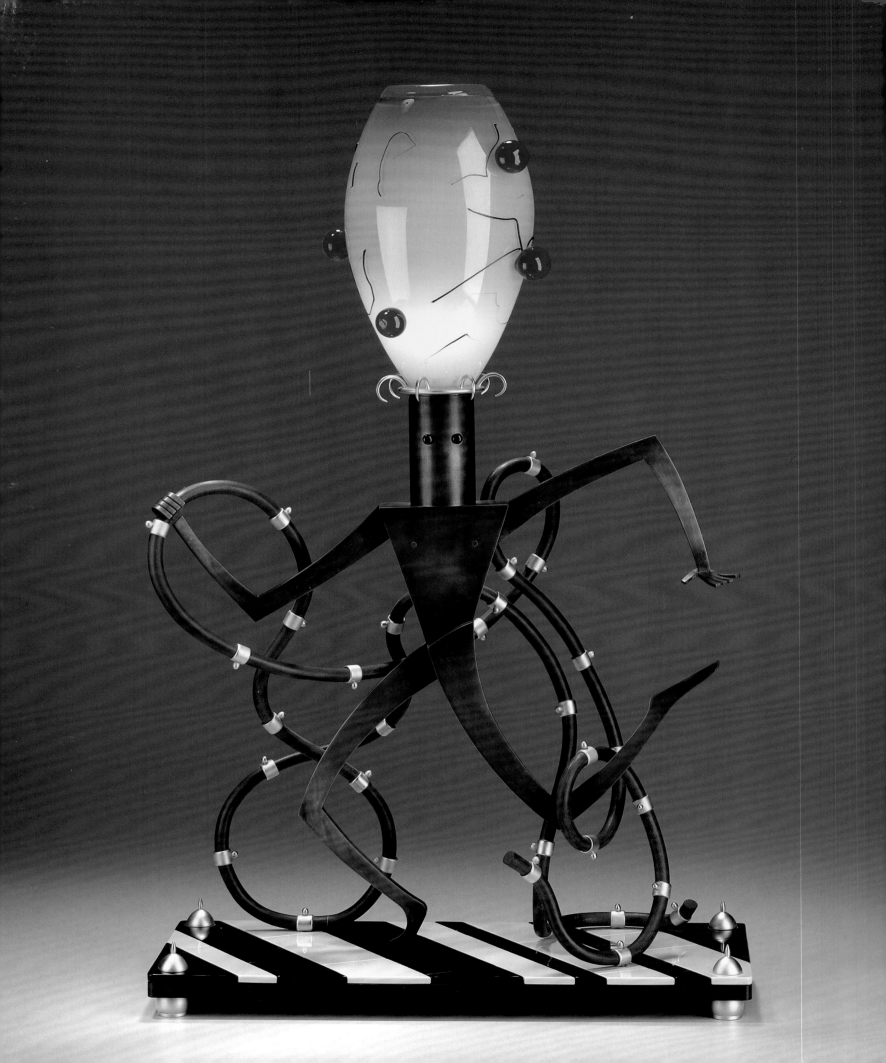

THE ART OF CRAFT

CONTEMPORARY WORKS FROM THE SAXE COLLECTION

TIMOTHY ANGLIN BURGARD

FINE ARTS MUSEUMS OF SAN FRANCISCO

This book has been published in conjunction with the exhibition *The Art of Craft: Contemporary Works from the Saxe Collection.*

Fine Arts Museums of San Francisco
M. H. de Young Memorial Museum
26 June–17 October 1999

The Art of Craft: Contemporary Works from the Saxe Collection has been organized by the Fine Arts Museums of San Francisco. Published with the assistance of the Andrew W. Mellon Foundation Endowment for Publications.

First published in the United States of America in paperback in 1999 by the Fine Arts Museums of San Francisco. First published in hardcover in 1999 by Bulfinch Press, Little, Brown and Company.

Library of Congress Catalogue Card Number 99-072626

ISBN 0-88401-098-8 (paperback)
ISBN 0-8212-2637-1 (hardcover)

Bulfinch Press is an imprint and trademark of Little, Brown and Company (Inc.)

Printed and bound in Hong Kong

Front Cover: William Morris, *Artifact: Tooth* (detail), 1996
Back Cover: Paul Soldner, *#976,* 1997
Spine: Kiki Smith, *Untitled* (detail), 1993

Frontispiece: Dan Dailey, *Rope Dancer,* 1995
Title Page: Kay Sekimachi, *Leaf Vessel XXIV* and *Leaf Vessel XXV,* 1997
Page 68: Dale Chihuly, *Prussian Green Macchia Pair with Cadmium Yellow Lip Wrap* (detail), 1968
Page 130: Richard DeVore, *#782* (detail), 1995
Page 188: Ron Fleming, *Alhambra* (detail), 1997
Page 222: Lia Cook, *Shadow Frieze* (detail), 1990
Page 248: Susan Colquitt, *Vespertine* (detail), 1992

CONTENTS

FOREWORD

It is with great pleasure and profound gratitude that the Fine Arts Museums of San Francisco present this selection of over 220 works from the Dorothy and George Saxe Collection of contemporary crafts. This exhibition celebrates the extraordinary generosity of the Saxes, whose promised gift of nearly 600 works will transform the Fine Arts Museums into one of the most important repositories of contemporary crafts in the United States. It also reaffirms the Museums' ongoing commitment to the exhibition and acquisition of works from both historical and contemporary craft movements. Earlier exhibitions at the Museums have ranged from historical surveys such as *The Art of Louis Comfort Tiffany* (1981) to contemporary subjects such as *Arneson and Politics* (1993). Recent acquisitions by the Museums include works by Robert Arneson, Lia Cook, Stephen De Staebler, Sam Maloof, and Manuel Neri, all of whom are represented in the Saxe Collection. Our contemporary fiber and wearable art collections have grown and diversified under the capable direction of Melissa Leventon, Curator of Textiles since 1986, who has deftly integrated the history of textiles into broader cultural contexts.

In 1979 the Corning Museum of Glass organized the exhibition *New Glass: A Worldwide Survey,* which traveled to San Francisco in 1981. This exhibition proved to be the original catalyst for the Saxe Collection; the Saxes began acquiring glass intensively at that time and have since formed one of the premier collections of contemporary crafts in the United States. Their interest in acquiring "art made using craft materials" has produced a collection of extraordinary quality, depth, and diversity. Similarly, their fore-sight in supporting the gallery system as an important compo-nent of studio craft's infrastructure has fostered greater public recognition of individual artists. Through their philanthropic involvement as trustees of cultural institutions, including the Pilchuck Glass School, the California College of Arts and Crafts, and The Jewish Museum of San Francisco, the Saxes have pioneered the integration of the studio craft movement into wider artistic, academic, and museum contexts. The Saxes have consistently led by example; the *Still Life* by Flora Mace and Joey Kirkpatrick featured in this exhibition was purchased specifically for donation to the Museums, and is already one of the high-lights of our permanent collection.

We are indebted to many individuals for bringing this super-lative exhibition and book to fruition. M. Lee Fatherree, principal photographer, brought his artistic expertise to bear upon the incredible diversity of objects in the collection; Ed Marquand and Susan E. Kelly of Marquand Books created the elegant book design; and Robin Kvietys, George Saxe's assistant, provided essen-tial information from the Saxe's extensive research files. Steven A. Nash, Associate Director of Museums and Chief Curator, provided support for this project from its inception; Elisabeth Cornu and Leslie Bone provided expert conservation of the collection; Anu Vaalas Schmidt compiled the book bibliography; Ann Karlstrom and Karen Kevorkian edited the manuscript with their usual skill and tact and oversaw the shaping of the book; Bill White and his

staff designed and installed this visually stunning exhibition; Kathe Hodgson coordinated the exhibition logistics with her usual aplomb; and Jane Glover ably provided assistance in manuscript preparation.

This book reflects the interdisciplinary vision of Timothy Anglin Burgard, the Ednah Root Curator of American Art and curator of this exhibition. His belief—that these works merit seri-ous art-historical consideration within a larger cultural context—helped to secure the promised gift of the Saxe Collection and is reflected in the scholarly essay accompanying this book.

Our greatest debt, however, is to Dorothy and George Saxe for their pioneering role in the contemporary crafts movement. The lasting impact of this exhibition will resonate not only through the promised gift of their collection to the Museums but also through the Dorothy and George Saxe Endowment Fund, which will ensure that their vision is perpetuated through future acquisitions. As we look forward to the new millennium and the construction of the new M. H. de Young Memorial Museum, we are indebted to the Saxes for providing us with a major building block for the future.

HARRY S. PARKER III
Director of Museums

7

TIMOTHY ANGLIN BURGARD

BEARERS OF MEANING

Cultural historians reviewing the second half of the twentieth century in the United States undoubtedly will observe that one of the more interesting art-world developments was the evolution of the "contemporary crafts movement." This extraordinary proliferation of objects in all media was paralleled, it will be noted, by a protracted and self-conscious debate over the definition and application of the terms *art* and *craft.* Future historians are less likely to resolve the debate than to question the validity and usefulness of these historically determined terms. Indeed, the perception of art and craft as distinct, or even contradictory, concepts validates assumptions that it ought instead to question.

While "art" is often viewed as a distinguishing trait of human cultures that has existed since prehistoric times, the specialized definition and perception of art—as objects conceived and created exclusively for aesthetic contemplation—is a relatively recent cultural creation, one largely defined by Europe and the United States. Similarly, despite their extended parallel (and often congruent) histories, attempts to segregate "craft"—as a distinct category of objects defined primarily by their supposedly utilitarian function—may reveal more about the desire to elevate and validate art than the inherent properties of craft objects.

Such definitions establish a false dichotomy by failing to recognize that every art or craft object has a "use," even if it is not a physical use but rather a cultural one, as a signifier of political, social, economic, or cultural orientation. While definitions of the terms *art* and *craft* are relevant to fields such as art history, historiography, aesthetics, and museology, they are of limited use in determining how these objects function within a given cultural context. A more productive approach might view all objects as manifestations of a complex matrix of cultural interchange—as bearers of meaning that reflect the time, place, and culture of their creation.

Fig. 1. Dale Chihuly
Left: *Early Cylinder,* 1975, blown glass, 7 × 4 in. diameter
Right: *Early Cylinder,* 1975, blown glass, 9¹⁄₁₆ × 6⅛ in. diameter

DALE CHIHULY—CRAFT IN CONTEXT

Dale Chihuly is perhaps the most internationally famous artist associated with the contemporary crafts movement, yet his glass works typically are discussed almost exclusively in aesthetic or technical terms. In fact, the roots of both Chihuly's convention-shattering aesthetics and technique, as well as the content of his works, may be traced in part to his involvement with some of the prominent countercultural issues of the late 1960s and early 1970s.

In 1970, while Chihuly was head of the glass department at the Rhode Island School of Design, he and John Landon erected a large billboard in Providence that bore a statement many readers assumed had been made by Richard Nixon during his 1968 presidential election campaign. Only at the end of this nationalistic, "law and order" quote did readers have their assumptions about its authorship contradicted by the words "Adolf Hitler, 1932."[1] A year later, as opposition to the Vietnam War spread to college campuses across the United States, Chihuly and fellow artists Italo Scanga and James Carpenter collaborated on an artistic antiwar statement for which they blew molten glass into a coffin-shaped bamboo mold.[2] While this less public and largely symbolic act of protest may have been of limited efficacy, it reflected the widespread belief that artists with a social conscience could not remain disengaged from contemporary events affecting humanity.

Like many artists of his generation, Chihuly's antiestablishment political stance was complemented by an alternative, utopian social vision. This vision found expression in 1971, when Chihuly founded the Pilchuck Glass School on land donated by John and Anne Gould Hauberg in the rural town of Stanwood, Washington. Pilchuck pioneer Toots Zynsky notes that the choice of a western location symbolized a conscious rejection of the eastern art establishment: "The philosophy behind it [Pilchuck] was that we were going West.... We went West with the idea that we might not come back.... It was the time of alternative education, when institutions were being questioned and analyzed."[3] Chihuly has observed that his choice of an unimproved site was unconventional, "because we were turning down farm buildings, electricity, and telephones. It was all part of this 'back to the earth' movement."[4] Reflecting the tenor of the times, one group of artists lobbied (unsuccessfully) to transform Pilchuck from a glass school into a multimedia art commune.[5]

This countercultural component of Pilchuck Glass School also was expressed through a shared fascination with Native American culture. The name "Pilchuck," chosen by Chihuly, is derived from the Chinook Indian words for "red" and "water," a reference to the iron-rich and rust-tinted waters of the nearby Pilchuck River.[6] One of the first structures erected on the Pilchuck site was John Landon's Sioux-style tipi, a communal gathering spot where the painter Robert Hendrikson, who called himself "White Eagle," introduced the Pilchuck community to Native American spiritualism and an ecological sensitivity to the natural environment.[7] These interests mirrored in microcosm a broader national interest in Native American issues.

Influential national events that coincided with the early years of Pilchuck included the occupation of San Francisco's Alcatraz

Fig. 2. Unidentified Navajo artist, *Double Saddle Blanket*, ca. 1885–90, wool and dyes, 53 × 33¼ in., Fine Arts Museums of San Francisco, gift of Andy Williams, 77.18.26

Fig. 3. Unidentified Maya artist (Petén, Guatemala), *Polychromed Beaker*, A.D. 600, earthenware with orange, white, black, red, and blue slip, Fine Arts Museums of San Francisco, Museum purchase, 78.41

ancient Native American ceramic vessels created by the Maya (fig. 3). Chihuly's Navajo blanket motifs were inspired by several experiences, including his creation of glass weavings while studying at the University of Washington (1960–61, 1963–65); an Andy Warhol exhibition at the Rhode Island School of Design entitled *Raid the Icebox* (1970), which incorporated Navajo blankets drawn from RISD's permanent collection; his teaching experience at the Institute of American Indian Art, Santa Fe (1974); and an exhibition of Navajo blankets at the Museum of Fine Arts, Boston (1975). Chihuly exhibited the *Navajo Blanket Cylinders* at the Institute in 1975, and again in 1976 in conjunction with a selection of actual Navajo blankets at Brown University's Bell Gallery.

Chihuly's second major series, the *Pilchuck Baskets*, was inspired by a 1977 visit to the Washington State Historical Museum in his hometown of Tacoma. Viewing the Museum's collection of Northwest Coast Indian baskets, Chihuly was struck by their organic forms, complex surface patterns, and the way in which their symmetrical forms had been distorted by weight and gravity as they were stacked together for storage. Chihuly's *Black Set* (fig. 4; p. 67) of 1980 also recalls the luminous blackware pottery (fig. 5) of the Southwest Pueblos. This type of pottery was refined

Island by Native American activists (1969–71), which Marlon Brando supported by declining his Best Actor Oscar for Francis Ford Coppola's film *The Godfather* (1970); the publication of Dee Brown's *Bury My Heart at Wounded Knee* (1970); and the occupation of Wounded Knee, South Dakota, by the American Indian Movement (1973). These serious political issues were paralleled in popular culture by the famous television commercial in which Iron Eyes Cody shed a single tear in an antilitter campaign (1970) and the general proliferation of a market for Native American crafts, especially Navajo blankets, Pueblo pottery, and Navajo and Zuni silver and turquoise jewelry. Given this context, it is revealing to observe that two of Chihuly's earliest series of works were inspired by Native American craft traditions.

Chihuly's first major glass series, the *Navajo Blanket Cylinders* (fig. 1; p. 8) of 1975–76, translated the woven patterns and textures of Navajo blankets (fig. 2) into glass by fusing glass-thread "drawings" by Kate Elliot and Flora C. Mace to the molten glass. These cylinders bear a remarkable structural resemblance to

Fig. 4. Dale Chihuly, *Black Set*, 1980, blown glass, 6¾ × 16 × 15 in.

Fig. 5. Maria Montoya Martinez (1887–1980) and Santana Martinez (b. 1909)
Left: *Bowl*, ca. 1960, ceramic, 3½ × 9¼ in. diameter, bequest of George Frederic Ward to the Fine Arts Museums of San Francisco, 1987.21.5
Right: *Bowl*, ca. 1960, ceramic, 2½ × 7 in., bequest of George Frederic Ward to the Fine Arts Museums of San Francisco, 1987.21.8

and transformed into a marketable commodity by the San Ildefonso potter Maria Montoya Martinez (1887–1980), whose growing popularity during the 1960s and 1970s helped to secure her reputation as the most famous Native American artist.

Chihuly's artistic embrace of Navajo blankets, Northwest Coast baskets, and Pueblo pottery, like his Pilchuck experience, can be viewed within a broader context in which Native American culture and politics entered the consciousness (and conscience) of mainstream EuroAmerican society. These Native American craft traditions were among the first to be appreciated and actively purchased for their aesthetic qualities by EuroAmericans in the late nineteenth century and are among the most popular to this day. The appeal of Native American objects, which were perceived as preserving prehistoric archetypes while also prefiguring the abstraction of modernism, was greatly enhanced by their powerful cultural associations. During the 1960s and 1970s, EuroAmericans in search of universal cultural values often turned to Native American cultures as sources of inspiration. These indigenous cultures appeared to preserve unbroken traditions of myth, spirituality, communal responsibility, environmental sensitivity, and artistic creation, and thus to provide modern EuroAmerican viewers (and artists) with access to the primordial roots of a collective past.

It is revealing that the most international of contemporary glass artists, one known for his appropriation and reinterpretation of Italian, Persian, and Japanese cultural traditions, founded his career on indigenous Native American craft traditions. By rejecting EuroAmerican ideological and artistic conventions and embracing alternative Native American models in his early works, Chihuly was able to create a new paradigm for the field of American glass art, one that retained an aura of antiestablishment and countercultural associations through its appropriation and assimilation of a wide range of cultural traditions.

BERTIL VALLIEN—THE GLASS KINGDOM

Bertil Vallien trained as a ceramist and industrial designer at Stockholm's Konstfack School of Arts, Crafts, and Design, which promoted traditional Swedish design virtues such as technical consistency, productivity, and marketability at the expense of individual artistic expression. Vallien's interest in alternative models of studio practice was sparked during a two-year stay (1961–63) in the Americas. In Los Angeles, Vallien first encountered the work of Peter Voulkos, whose innovative ceramic sculptures had a liberating effect upon his own subsequent work. Vallien also traveled extensively in Mexico, and the country's extraordinary ancient art and architectural history provided a precedent for his later exploration of Sweden's ancient Viking heritage.[8]

Since his return to Sweden in 1963, Vallien has worked at the Åfors Glassworks (now merged with the firm of Kosta Boda) in the province of Småland, a region popularly known as "The Glass Kingdom" for its numerous glass companies and studios. When the economic survival of these firms was threatened by foreign competition in the 1970s, Vallien publicly argued that salvation lay in the creation of art glass, rather than in increased reliance on mechanization. Putting his artistic philosophy into practice, Vallien played a major role in fostering a Swedish glass renaissance, a communal enterprise more reminiscent of traditional craft guilds than modern industrial factories.[9]

Vallien's pioneering and innovative use of sand casting, a technique with ancient origins that today is more commonly associated with heavy industry, may be viewed as a conscious rebellion against the highly finished products valued by the traditional Swedish glass industry. Like Peter Voulkos's innovative ceramics, Vallien's sand-cast glass also transcends traditional media-based craft definitions by synthesizing sculpture, painting (powdered-glass pigments), and assemblage (the inclusion of precast glass and nonglass objects).

Vallien's technical innovations were paralleled by a renewed social commitment inspired by the cataclysmic events of 1968 in the United States and Europe. In an interview during that year, Vallien stated his politicized view of the artist's newly transformed role in contemporary society: "Today the only justification for an artist-craftsman is as a ploughshare: to have a meaning, to disturb and inspire—not just satisfy a desire for possessions."[10]

Vallien's desire to create works that had meaning and the power "to disturb and inspire" led him to Sweden's ancient Viking heritage and its potent legacy of history, legend, and myth. Historically, the word *Viking* specifically designated sea pirates or raiders, and this singular association of the Vikings with seafaring culture persists in the popular imagination. At their height from the eighth to the eleventh centuries, Viking trade routes and settlements stretched from the Nordic homeland east to Russia and west to Great Britain and even America, thus transcending current national borders and forging a collective identity for Nordic cultures. Transcending strict religious definitions through its gradual conversion to Christianity, Viking culture created a remarkable fusion of pagan and Christian beliefs and iconography that is vaguely familiar to contemporary viewers, while providing a link to a lost past.

Given the centrality of seafaring in Scandinavian culture, Vallien's sand-cast glass ships inevitably evoke ancient associations with the epic voyages of myth and legend, of sunken ships and their cargoes buried beneath the sea, and of ships that have been removed from their natural element and sealed in burial mounds. Specific Viking precedents for Vallien's ship theme include the famous Oseberg ship burial (ca. 834) in Vestfold, on the west coast of Oslo Fjord in Norway. Buried beneath a large mound, the ship burial chamber contained the bodies of two women and their funerary goods, which included food, utensils, animals, and transportation—a ritual gathering of the prosaic necessities of everyday life for use in the eternal afterlife.[11]

Other possible sources of inspiration include the boat-shaped alignments of standing stones throughout Scandinavia and the late-eighth- to early-ninth-century Viking "picture stones" on the island of Gotland, Sweden, whose most common motifs are ships, male equestrians, women riding in carts, and depictions of Asgard (home of the gods) or Valhalla (the hall of heroes). The presence of actual ships, horses, and carts in burial mounds has led scholars to interpret these objects as symbols of the journey of the deceased to the afterlife.[12]

Vallien's *Bellagio* (fig. 6; p. 122) of 1993, cast in transparent glass that has been tinted blue by powdered pigments, appears less like a ship than like the water that would be displaced by its hull. Frozen in time and suspended in space, this symbolic vessel has

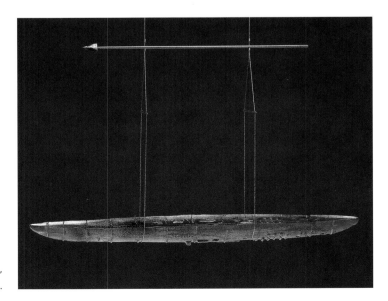

Fig. 6. Bertil Vallien, *Bellagio*, 1993, sand-cast glass, steel, and wire, 33 (vessel and arrow) × 53 × 8 in.

Fig. 8. Bertil Vallien, *Head 35*, 1997, sand-cast glass, 70¾ × 13¾ × 13¾ in.

no actual maritime counterpart, no clear bow or stern, and no visible means of propulsion. Vallien has described his ship form as a protective, womblike "Mother-symbol," a conception that is reinforced by the diminutive human figure that appears to be floating or swimming within the hull.[13] Also encased within *Bellagio*'s protective hull, as if submerged or entombed, are a seemingly random accumulation of glass and metal objects and symbols, including crosses, arrows, birds, stairs, ladders/rigging, striated columnar bars, a wrench, a piece of wire mesh screen mounted like a sail on a mast, a steel plate with rivetlike protrusions, a red sunlike form, and a human mask.

Like the conjunction of ships and other symbols on Viking rune stones, *Bellagio*'s evocative images encourage the creation of a narrative but defy decoding. These embedded signs and symbols, shaped by stream of consciousness and subconscious dream states, suggest direction, movement, and linkage, but resist attachment to any specific set of beliefs from the past or present (as even collective beliefs are transformed by the unique perceptions of individuals). Vallien notes that the meaning and interpretation

of his vessels are variable and unfathomable: "I choose the words, but do not consciously choose their arrangements, the sentences which materialize have certainly no counterpart in my mind; they occur quite by chance."[14] While their point of origin and final destination remain uncertain, Vallien's ships are linked by their common themes of voyage and passage—from the past, through the present, and into the future; and from birth, through life, and into death.

Vallien's *Head 34* (fig. 7; p. 119) and *Head 35* (fig. 8; p. 118), both of 1997, were inspired by a magazine account of a thirteen-year-old Swedish girl named Carolina, who, after a fall, entered a seemingly irreversible coma in 1876. When she miraculously reawakened in 1907, in complete possession of her senses, she recounted that she had found herself in infinite darkness, surrounded by blue men.[15] Carolina's extraordinary firsthand account of a realm between the conscious and the unconscious, between life and death, paralleled Vallien's own interest in transitional states of being. He subsequently created a series of three-dimensional

Fig. 7. Bertil Vallien, *Head 34*, 1997, sand-cast glass, 70¾ × 13¾ × 13¾ in.

heads that attempted to give visual form to Carolina's experience of interior and exterior worlds, and the intangible line that separates these realms.

Although created as a series, each of Vallien's *Heads* is differentiated by its form and content. They explore the similarities and differences that define individual and collective humanity. Mounted on totemic wooden shafts that allude to human bodies, the *Heads* confront their viewers at eye level and encourage mutual recognition. As in his earlier series of masklike *Faces*, Vallien's reductive vocabulary accentuates the expressive power of these heads, straddling the line between the naturalistic and the abstract.

The mouth and nose of *Head 34* are partially obscured by a superimposed T shape that resembles the abstracted facial features found in "ethnographic" masks or Cubist sculptures. The right-angled rigidity of the T speaks of the human desire to impose a rational order upon the exterior world. This geometric order is undermined by a small, isolated X or cross mark on the left forehead that may refer to Carolina's accidental, coma-inducing wound. Additional X-marks on the back of the head may represent the scars of either physical or emotional experience, or stars, suggesting that the interior of the human mind is as vast and unfathomable as the universe. The analogy is reinforced by the planetary sphere and celestial concentric circles that are visible through the polished side and back surfaces of the head.

Head 34 also contains a small, standing figure surrounded by the schematic outline of a house. This conjunction of house and human evokes the universal idea of home as a fixed point of reference in every individual's personal memory and cosmology. It also suggests an analogy between the house as the shelter of the physical human body and the head as the locus of its spirit. The fragile and vulnerable nature of this spirit is conveyed by the compression of Vallien's *Heads* into smaller-than-life, egglike forms that have been shorn of extraneous naturalistic detail. Their delicate, membranelike surfaces, penetrable by light, convey the absence of a substantial protective barrier between the exterior and the interior of these heads. In a very real sense they are not representations of physical anatomy but of the metaphysical mind.

The surface of *Head 35* lacks facial features and is instead covered with an X-shaped pattern of pinpoint protrusions that resembles ritual scarification (rather than the random X-wound of *Head 34*). The actual human face is revealed through an oval aperture that resembles an incision or a lesion, an eye, or even the silhouette of one of Vallien's boats. Like Vallien's earlier masklike *Faces*, the *Heads* hint that our faces are merely physical facades and that our true identities lie within the infinite depths of the human mind and spirit. Bathed in an eerie blue glow, the moonlike human face visible through the aperture of *Head 35* evokes overlapping references to Carolina's coma, the mental voyage of nocturnal sleep and dream states, as well as larger connections to cyclical lunar phases and cosmic forces.

Vallien's *Map* series provides an extended conceptual exploration of maps and mapmaking as metaphors for the innate desire of humans to orient themselves cosmologically. Mounted vertically, they are scored with grid patterns similar to notations of longitude and latitude on a flat surface and are surrounded by black-and-white borders that resemble the mileage-scale bars on maps. Vallien's *Maps* are characterized by ambiguous spatial and perspectival relationships that blur the distinction between plan and section, or between aerial and perspective views. Fusing perspectival painting and low-relief sculpture, their topographic surfaces are actually embedded with the objects being mapped, a tactile solution to the difficulties inherent in mapping three-dimensional experience in two dimensions. Their sequential numerical designations clearly identify the maps as sections of a larger whole, without revealing the identity or the scale of the larger entity being mapped.

Vallien's *Map* series had its origins in a newspaper photograph that was pinned to the wall of the artist's studio for several years. When Vallien went to discard the faded clipping and read the caption for the first time, he realized that the photograph he had always perceived as the abstracted face of a man was actually an aerial view of a bomb-desolated village in Iraq:

> One could make out an ordered system of roads leading off the circular marketplace, remains of houses and walls enclosing small fields. A settlement which had been laboriously built up over hundreds of years into its present

form. Now, razed to the ground in a matter of seconds by a deed of animosity. Knowing the true significance of the picture made me feel bad. Bad about how erroneously I had constructed it. All I had seen was a decorative pattern of graphic marks, which I imagined to be the face of a man staring straight at me. The picture assumed a special significance and prompted an exhibition—entitled *Area II*. The theme of which is an archaeological excavation.[16]

Vallien's *Area II* installation was comprised of the *Maps* (square glass reliefs with embedded objects), *Finds* (glass cubes with encased objects), and *Watchers* (suspended icicle- or swordlike forms). Their extended commentary on culture, history, and archaeology was accentuated by the exhibition setting—the ruins of seventeenth-century Borgholms Castle on Öland.

The central mass of *Map IV* (fig. 9; p. 120) of 1998 resembles an archaeological cross section of an enormous burial mound, or one of the ancient American stepped pyramids that Vallien would have seen during his travels in Mexico in 1963. The pyramid association is reinforced by the two staircases along the lower edge that once provided points of entry, but are now obscured by accumulated debris. Embedded within this pyramidal mound are at least four rows of masks with human features, arranged edge to edge and layered like accumulated votive offerings. To the right

are additional layers of protruding objects reminiscent of the stacked, cylindrical amphorae often uncovered in ancient archaeological sites. The cut length of bound-wire cable embedded within the mound, like a ship or bridge cable or a telecommunications link, serves as a symbol of severed connection and communication. The metal ring attached at the lower right is suggestive of a boat mooring in an ancient harbor, or perhaps is a punning reference to the pull on a schoolroom map.

Surmounting the pyramidal mound is a fragmentary, masklike human head, cradled by two hands. Superimposed on this head is a large Y, a form that Vallien utilized in his series of masklike *Faces* to represent an abstracted human nose and eyes. The Y also resembles a fork in the road, or a divining rod, and contains a terrestrial/celestial sphere, all of which are evocative symbols for directional choice and guidance. Within an archaeological context, it is possible to view the masklike head, placed atop a pyramid, as a divine mediator for an ancient culture. However, elaborating upon his description of the *Area II* installation as "an imaginary archaeological excavation," Vallien has written that "It consists of a series of *Maps*, and *Finds* of glass or ice, from a site that has been exposed to a most terrible catastrophe: volcanic heat, nuclear explosion, or the abysmal cold of the Antarctic. The man with the menacing stare [from the newspaper photograph of the bombed Iraqi village], however, remained in the maps. As an image of evil."[17]

Given this catastrophic, even apocalyptic context, it is possible to posit alternate interpretations of Vallien's multivalent imagery in which the etched quadrants might be viewed as the sectors of a military map, the piled cylindrical vessels as munitions, the cable as a fuse, the metal ring as a hand grenade pin, and the open-mouthed masks as screaming human beings. A targetlike form at the lower center and a vivid yellow coffin shape at the lower left (with a cross concealed on the verso) reinforce this potential reading. The masklike head and the pyramidal mound may be viewed as Vallien's anthropomorphic embodiment of evil.

Fig. 9. Bertil Vallien, *Map IV*, 1998, sand-cast glass, steel, and copper, 26 × 30 × 10 in., on a steel base 15⅜ × 27⅜ × 9¹³⁄₁₆ in.

Fig. 10. William Morris, *Petroglyph Urn with Horn*, 1989–90, blown glass, 24⅜ × 33 × 6½ in., on a steel stand 20¼ × 23 × 5 in.

This mutated or mutilated head-and-shoulders bust has the compound eye and clawlike protuberances of an insect, and wears the small human masks and bound-wire cable upon his chest like the medals and decorative braid on a military officer's uniform.

Like Picasso's *Guernica*, Vallien's *Maps* were inspired by a specific historical incident in which an ancient town built up over centuries was destroyed in minutes by a massive aerial bombardment. However, these works also pose a universal question regarding humankind's destructive impulses, which represent an inversion and perversion of the rational thought that produces maps. As in Vallien's *Masque Why* (1996), the directional or divinatory Y of *Map IV* may also be interpreted as the encompassing, interrogative "Why?"

As an artist, Vallien has been inspired by the cumulative layering of history that builds upon the foundations of the past, a past that he has productively excavated and mined for use in the present. In *Map IV*, he implicitly poses the question of what the future archaeological excavation of our own culture will reveal—preservation or destruction, civilization or nuclear apocalypse, buried art or buried munitions? Vallien's hope for the future is perhaps concealed on the verso of *Map IV* (see p. 121), where there are five human figures with outstretched arms and legs. Two float in isolation, while two others have joined hands. The fifth figure with outstretched arms and legs is contained within an embryonic, boat-shaped, yellow oval. Escaping from the present and floating upward into the blue firmament of stars formed by the intersecting map grids, this figure suggests that salvation lies in our collective humanity.

WILLIAM MORRIS—THE GLASS AGE

William Morris's fascination with the historical past may be traced to his vivid childhood recollections of digging pot shards from Indian burial mounds, finding arrowheads in caves, and, in a particularly memorable experience, discovering "a beautiful flint point" while hiking in the Sierra Nevada Mountains.[18] As a young artist, these primeval experiences were reinforced by trips to Great Britain and France, where Morris was inspired by the megaliths of the Orkney Islands and Stonehenge, as well as Stone Age cave paintings.[19] Morris's subsequent glass work encompasses a unique vision of prehistory and history—including primitive petroglyphs, paintings, sculptural objects, functional tools, objects of ritual belief and their spirits, and the remains of human and animal presences. Emulating artists of the ancient past, Morris has created a realm populated by primitive people and animals, and animated by elemental natural forces and instinctual human drives and desires.

Morris's suspended *Petroglyph Urn with Horn* of 1989–90, an organic, pouchlike glass vessel suspended from a glass animal horn, is decorated with powdered-glass-pigment drawings reminiscent of the famous cave paintings of Lascaux, France, and Altamira, Spain. Morris's title reinforces the analogy, suggesting that these images are drawn on a rock rather than fused in glass. One side of the vessel (fig. 10; p. 91) depicts a diminutive hunter taking aim with a bow and arrow at an enormous elklike animal who rears on his hind legs and threatens to crush his adversary. The scale of this animal hints at its power for the hunter. The other side (see p. 90) depicts four of these animals gathered parallel as if in a herd, while three of their number gallop like constellations across a blue firmament. The inversion of the figure/ground

Fig. 11. William Morris, *Canopic Jar—Buck,* 1993, blown glass, 37¾ × 12½ in.

relationship on the two sides of the vessel (sky-blue elk on stonelike ground vs. stonelike elk on sky-blue ground) may represent the interconnectedness of all creation, as well as the transmutation and animals (and occasionally humans) from physical flesh to immaterial spirit during the life-and-death struggle of the hunt.

Petroglyph Urn with Horn resembles a crucible-like vessel suspended on a spit over a fire, its bright orange horn and rim glowing as if superheated. The resemblance provides a particularly apt visual metaphor for glass, which originates in the element of fire, as well as for the centrality of fire as a necessity for survival and sustenance during the Stone Age. The vessel's surface, animated by the vivid powdered pigments and sparkling gold inclusions, re-creates the experience of viewing cave paintings illuminated by firelight. However, the true function of *Petroglyph Urn with Horn* may be ritualistic—to commemorate the spirits of the animals that provided its constituent parts. Suspended above the ground, the animal-covered vessel is freed from the earthbound realm and elevated to a higher realm of animist, spiritual belief.

The theme of the hunt is further explored in Morris's *Canopic Jar—Buck* (fig. 11; p. 92) of 1993, which reproduces the form of ancient Egyptian canopic jars—stone, ceramic, or wooden funerary containers created to hold the organs of the deceased (fig. 12). Popular throughout the Pharaonic period, canopic jars played an important role in the mummification process, and were usually produced in sets of four to hold the deceased individual's embalmed liver, lungs, stomach, and intestines. These organs, thought to be essential for survival in the afterlife, fell under the protection of four minor deities, the Sons of Horus. Imsety, who took human form, protected the liver; Hapy, a baboon, protected the lungs; Duamutef, a jackal, protected the stomach; and Qebehsenuf, a falcon, protected the intestines.

Fig. 12. Unidentified Egyptian artist, *Canopic Jar of Pa-et-heri-neter,* late Dynastic Period, 747–332 B.C., alabaster, Fine Arts Museums of San Francisco, estate of M. H. de Young, 20298.4a–b

Morris's canopic jar does not depict one of the four traditional Egyptian deities, but rather a North American buck, and is inextricably linked to his own experiences as a hunter of this animal. Morris has hunted since he was a teenager and habitually takes the first month of hunting season as his only vacation.[20] His seemingly anachronistic use of the "primitive" bow and arrow links him to the ritualistic hunts of his prehistoric predecessors and provides firsthand experience of the life-and-death struggles that have lost their resonance for consumers who purchase processed and packaged meat in a supermarket.

Morris's *Canopic Jar—Buck* is a sensitive appropriation of its ancient prototype, which has been resurrected and reinterpreted for new rituals. The illusionistic *craquelure* of the jar augments its associations with age and ossification, and evokes a fragmented object from antiquity that has been pieced together by archaeologists. The matte blue surface replicates the appearance of Egyptian faience ceramics and sublimates the seductive surface properties of glass in favor of this object's deeper meditations on life and death.

Morris notes that his hunts have fostered an altered and heightened state of awareness in relation to nature: "To me, each animal is like a special vessel, and I think about that when I hunt. When I first started hunting, I just wanted to get the guts out and get the meat home. It's not like that anymore—hunting is more like a ceremony to me now. That's one of the reasons I was attracted by the format of the Egyptian canopic jar, which was not only about death, but part of a ritual about the inner life of the spirit."[21]

Morris's *Canopic Jar—Buck* not only commemorates the likeness of his actual prey on the vessel lid, but also resurrects these animals pictorially on the body of the vessel. These anthropomorphic deer, perhaps human hunters who have donned deer heads and skins as camouflage, rise up on their hind legs and hunt their animal brethren with bows and arrows, thus linking the identities of the hunter and the hunted. Morris's fusion of an ancient Egyptian form with a contemporary animal suggests that perennial mysteries and truths regarding the hunt persist in the midst of our seemingly prosaic present.

Unlike Morris's pristine *Petroglyph Urn with Horn* or *Canopic Jar—Buck, Artifact Still Life* (fig. 13; p. 87) of 1989–90 resembles a newly unearthed archaeological cache. Upon closer examination, the identity of these "artifacts" is remarkably ambiguous. Do they represent a real or an imagined culture, an authentic archaeological excavation, or an artificial museum display in which the objects have been cleaned and rearranged on a pedestal for exhibition? Are the bones animal or human, from extant or extinct creatures, and remnants of a sacred burial site or an ancient domestic dwelling? Are these functional or ritual vessels, rudimentary wheels or cosmic circles? The glass surfaces are translucent and iridescent, like ancient glass that has deteriorated

Fig. 13. William Morris, *Artifact Still Life*, 1989–90, blown glass, scavo, gold leaf, and copper, 15¼ × 44 × 22 in.

chemically through burial or exposure to the elements, and yet none are cracked or broken.

Morris's doctor-father has observed that his son's glass bones are anatomically incorrect, a scientific critique rendered irrelevant by the emotional resonance of bones in the human imagination.[22] Morris's bones serve as emblems of mortality, a traditional *vanitas* or *memento mori* still-life theme that encourages meditations on the transitory nature of earthly existence and possessions, and the inevitability and finality of death. The conjunction of the vessels with bones makes explicit Morris's perception of human and animal bodies as merely physical "vessels" for the "inner life of the spirit," another common *vanitas* conceit. Ironically, like museum artifacts, these mortal remains have been endowed with a degree of permanence, if not immortality, through their transmutation into art.

Like a museum display, *Artifact Still Life* ostensibly offers contemporary viewers an authentic and tangible connection with their "primitive" origins and historical past. Although in actuality its components have no exact historical (or anatomical) equivalent, Morris has endowed this archaeological assemblage with an aura of authenticity that obscures its skillful artifice. His seemingly arbitrary, random collections of objects are emblematic of the fragmentary nature of the past and of the intensely personal nature of memory. Morris's "artifacts" are validated by the viewer's knowledge of historical prototypes, subliminal awareness of ancient archetypes, and by the human desire to order the world. These isolated objects encourage, even require, real or imagined narratives to explain their creation and survival, even as they demonstrate that all our perceptions of other cultures are artificial constructs grounded in our own belief systems.

Like Stone Age cave paintings that have been aestheticized through their elevation into high art, the beauty of Morris's objects often threatens to obscure their elemental themes of life, death, struggle, belief, and history. Through their graphic imagery, vivid colors, and technical virtuosity, Morris evokes, not specific ancient objects or archaeological artifacts, but rather the visceral emotions and sense of wonder experienced by Stone Age artists as they confronted the mysteries of nature.

Among these emotions is fear (of the known and the unknown)

—an instinctual human response that has been neutralized or negated in cave paintings and other Stone Age images by the application of post-Enlightenment rationalism. This scientific and technological bias is readily apparent in media-based definitions such as *Stone Age* and *Iron Age,* which were applied by historians—not by the makers, for whom materials were an expressive means, not a technological end.

Morris's works attempt to re-create an age that exists today largely in our collective unconscious—an age in which the eternal struggle between nature and humans was of uncertain outcome (with nature often holding the upper hand). Through his work, Morris suggests that it is not just nature's physical forces that have been described and harnessed by science, but that its spiritual forces have been demystified and suppressed. Forged in the fires of a modern Glass Age, Morris's work represents not simply an intellectual, archaeological, or museological exercise, but rather an attempt to reconnect contemporary viewers with these unseen, unknowable forces.

CLIFFORD RAINEY—CULTURAL CONSERVATION

The ostensible subject of Clifford Rainey's *Fetish* of 1990 (fig. 14; p. 127) is a Coca-Cola bottle, an instantly recognizable and distinctly American icon so internationally pervasive that its multivalent cultural connotations have become nearly transparent. The subject recalls Andy Warhol's silk-screened Coke bottles, which were mechanically reproduced and multiplied in order to draw an analogy between the commodification of commercial products and culture. However, while Rainey's Coke bottle is similarly an object of material culture recontextualized within the realm of art, it is a solitary and unique object, cast larger than its real-life counterpart, painstakingly handcrafted and embellished, and physically and conceptually deconstructed.

Rainey's physical deconstruction of the "hobble skirt" Coke bottle's voluptuous curves draws attention to its anthropomorphic characteristics and its potential as a modern metaphor for the human form. The visual resemblance to a classical column that has broken into its constituent segments and rusting iron support

Fig. 14. Clifford Rainey, *Fetish,* 1990, cast recycled glass,
iron nails, glass beads, wood, and oil paint,
39½ × 10 × 9½ in.

bottle thoughtlessly jettisoned from a passing private plane. While the protagonist of the film attempts to return the bottle to its rightful owner, Rainey envisions a more probable scenario of reinterpretation and assimilation within an existing cultural belief system.

Specifically, the inclusion of embedded iron nails in *Fetish* and the addition of a small beaded necklace around its neck suggest that this object has been transformed into an African power figure such as a Kongo *nkisi nkondi* (fig. 15). These carved wooden figures, perceived as living presences and conversed with by clients, play an important role in settling lawsuits or serious disputes within Kongo communities. The accumulated additions are of symbolic importance and include embedded nails representing condensed arguments presented in the course of a dispute or trial.

The original cultural context and purpose of such figures typically were ignored or misinterpreted by colonial collectors, who viewed their makers as "pagan" and pejoratively classified their

rods not only suggests that the Coke bottle is "classic," but that it shares anatomical analogies with the entasis or anthropomorphic curvature of ancient Greco-Roman columns.[23] These anthropomorphic associations are accentuated by the object's "tree trunk" support and its protruding appendage, which is reminiscent of a maple-sugar spout (an appropriate reference for sugar-sweetened soda), or a phallus, symbolizing sexual potency and fertility.

Rainey's conceptual deconstruction of the Coke bottle posits its cultural appropriation by contemporary African culture. This conceit provided the story line for director Jamie Uys's film *The Gods Must Be Crazy* (1984), in which an Aboriginal culture in Botswana is thrown into turmoil by the introduction of a Coke

Fig. 15. Unidentified artist (Kongo, coastal Zaire),
Nkisi Nkondi (Nail and Blade Oath-Taking Image),
19th century, wood, textile, iron, bronze, twigs, glass,
and horn, Fine Arts Museums of San Francisco,
Museum purchase, gift of Mrs. Paul L. Wattis and
The Fine Arts Museums Foundation, 1986.16.1

Fig. 16. Unidentified Native American artist, *Petroglyph*, sandstone, 33 × 20 in., Fine Arts Museums of San Francisco, gift of Erle Loran, 73.25.1

creations as "primitive" fetishes unworthy of aesthetic consideration. Only in the early twentieth century were these "ethnographic" objects selectively appropriated and redefined as "art" by avant-garde European and American artists, who promoted a perception that the most abstract of these works could transcend their ethnographic origins through their mutually validating association with modernism. This process of cultural redefinition has facilitated the separation of modernist "primitivism" from its origins in colonialism, as well as from related issues of politics, race, and sexuality.[24]

Fetish dissects and subverts these culturally determined definitions of art and ethnography, primitive and modern, naturalism and abstraction. Applying the sensibility and scrutiny of an anthropologist, the Irish-born Rainey suggests that the Coke bottle might properly be perceived as a uniquely American "fetish" or object of tribal ritual. This startling suggestion facilitates a recognition of other potential "fetishes" in the Western tradition, including "high art" religious subjects such as the martyrdom of Saint Sebastian pierced by arrows, a subject that Rainey has metaphorically incorporated into his work as a reference to the martyrdom of Northern Ireland during its political upheavals.[25]

Rainey, who witnessed British political colonialism firsthand in Belfast, Northern Ireland, also suggests that the Coke bottle, the most prominent symbol of the pervasive global influence of American culture and values, represents a new phenomenon—commercial colonialism. This connection is rendered explicit in Rainey's *Africa* (1991), whose central element is a Coke bottle, a now pervasive element of American "pop" culture in many African countries. While contemporary cultural debate in the United States has focused on the potentially divisive nature of identity-based art and culture, *Fetish* offers testament to the global Americanization and homogenization of culture. This process is likely to accelerate in the coming decades with the continued proliferation of American culture and values through technology, media, and the use of English (and the Coke bottle) as a global language.

The complex and reciprocal relationships that constitute contemporary cultural discourse—in an era in which people, objects, and ideas transcend traditional boundaries—illustrate the difficulty of fixing the identity and meaning of objects that are continually assimilated and redefined within new contexts. *Fetish* partially replicates the appearance of its Coke bottle model but, distorted and deconstructed in translation, it subverts conventional usage. Transformed into a ritual artifact like the *nkisi nkondi*, this cultural hybrid serves as mediating figure for a new global and cross-cultural context.

Rainey's fabrication of *Fetish* from recycled Coke bottles provides an apt metaphor, not only for the environmental conservation of recycled materials, but for the recycling of universal ideas and associations that persist over time in collective human consciousness.[26] This conception of cultural conservation is reinforced by the presence of hand-painted petroglyphs of a human figure and cosmic symbols on the inner surfaces of the deconstructed Coke bottle. These symbols resemble another American tradition, the prehistoric Native American petroglyphs (fig. 16) that were carved into the stratified cliffs of the American Southwest. Their superimposition on the stratified layers of fused Coke bottles in *Fetish* provides a cultural core sample that graphically illustrates the timeless human need to create images and objects that express and mediate our relationship to the world.

PETER VOULKOS—BREAKING WITH TRADITION

Since the 1950s, Peter Voulkos has created sculptures whose form, content, and scale have permanently shattered traditional "craft" definitions of the ceramic medium. Beginning in 1953, Voulkos's ceramics were transformed by his encounter with the Abstract Expressionists, who emphasized process, performance, and primal expression in their works. Emulating their example, Voulkos created unprecedented, large-scale, glazed and painted ceramic sculptures that transcended the traditional boundaries between paintings, sculpture, and ceramics. In subsequent works, Voulkos physically deconstructed and reconstructed traditional vessel forms such as the plate, tea bowl, or ice bucket, subverting or negating their functional uses or associations, and compelling their reinterpretation as art. He also has created new ceramic forms, such as his cylindrical "stacks," which lack any utilitarian function, and which serve as equivalents for the psychic and physical act of creation.

Voulkos's approach to art also has been strongly influenced by the teachings of Zen Buddhism, including a focus on means rather than ends, a receptiveness to chance and accident, and an interest in the expressive potential of the calligraphic gesture. The Japanese potter Shoji Hamada (1894–1978), whom Voulkos met in 1952, encouraged the younger artist to embrace a Zen approach to ceramics based not just upon a physical proficiency with materials and technique, but also upon a complete mental and spiritual fusion between the creator and the object created. Voulkos has frequently cited Hamada's statement that it took him ten years to learn the potter's wheel and another ten years to forget it, a philosophy that Voulkos aspired to in his early attempts to create a fully formed teapot in two minutes: "It made you aware of the fact that material, idea, and self would come together, transcending the object."[27]

Voulkos's ongoing fascination with the plate, another form associated with food presentation and consumption, would seem to be anachronistic, reinforcing the perception of ceramics as a purely functional craft medium. However, the conceptual and visual power of Voulkos's plates are partly predicated on the tension created between the intangible associations of the plate form and its physical deconstruction. Often formed with breaks and displaced or missing pieces, these plates encourage, but frustrate, the viewer's attempts to mentally mend or reassemble the fragments into a usable whole. By accentuating the physical structure of the plates, and a physical (rather than painterly) form of calligraphy composed of slashes, gouges, and incisions, Voulkos synthesized the painterly gesture with the physical act of sculpting.

Coincident with the creation of his first wood-fired ceramics in 1979, Voulkos developed a strong interest in the scholarly debate surrounding astronomical and archaeological subjects such as the origin of the universe and the mysteries of the Great Pyramids at Giza, Egypt.[28] The arcing, centrifugal spiral at the center of Voulkos's *Untitled (Plate)* of 1981 (fig. 17; p. 139) is an appropriate symbol for the creation of a plate thrown on a spinning potter's wheel, but it also resembles cosmic forms and may be related to larger conceptions of creation. Similarly, the circular holes that puncture the surface of the plate, along with the embedded white ceramic pebbles, resemble rudimentary depictions of stellar or planetary forms. The incised lines that link these forms are

Fig. 17. Peter Voulkos, *Untitled (Plate)*, 1981, stoneware, 4 × 20¼ in. diameter

suggestive of an attempt to apply organizing principles to these
seemingly random points—a visualization of terrestrial or celestial
coordinates or journeys.

These terrestrial and celestial associations are perhaps con-
joined in the central form that resembles a house with a pyramidal
roof. This architectonic form and the surrounding markings are
suggestive of an Egyptian pyramid's outer structure, inner chambers, and passageways, and perhaps their associated architectural
and cosmic axes.[29] The two impressed, rectangular forms, whose
manufactured, hard-edged geometry contrasts with the organic
linking lines, break through the organic perimeter of the plate and
are evocative of architectural ramps or points of entry.

For Voulkos, however, the architectural form of the pyramid is
secondary to its ritual function—as a shelter and a tomb, and as
a point of mediation between this life and the afterlife, between
mortality and immortality, and between the earth and the heavens. The imagery embedded within Voulkos's circular plate, which
resembles a terrestrial or celestial map or globe, is ultimately inde-
cipherable, yet affirms humankind's instinctual desire to define
its relationship to the cosmos.

Voulkos's greatest source of artistic inspiration has been Japan's
ceramic tradition, especially the extraordinary bowls created for
the Japanese tea ceremony known as Chado (way of tea). While
ritual tea drinking was practiced in Japan as early as the twelfth
century, it gradually was codified by Zen priests and court
connoisseurs into a ritual embodying the Buddhist reverence for
the beautiful in daily life. The aesthetic merits of Japanese tea
bowls formed a recognized element of the tea ceremony, and
connoisseurs particularly prized rustic bowls that repudiated the
ostentation and ornamentation of fine porcelain.

Many of these tea bowls were created at the pottery centers of
Shigaraki, Seto, Tamba, Tokoname, Bizen, and Eichizen (collectively
known as the "Six Ancient Kilns"). These kilns became famous
when their wares were adopted by Zen tea masters, who appreciated the structural and surface imperfections as visual counterparts to the philosophical embrace of naturalness and chance.[30]

These unconventional tea bowls provided Voulkos with an important prototype for objects whose aesthetic forms contravened
ceramic conventions, and whose ritual significance is as important
as their ostensible function.

According to Voulkos, his "ice bucket" forms bridge the "difference in space and thought" between his own small tea bowls and
his large "stacks." Voulkos's *Untitled (Ice Bucket)* of 1983 (fig. 18;
p. 138) appears to have been formed naturally through an accumulation of geological strata. Its hourglass form visually conveys
a sense of support, weight, and compression and accentuates the
base (beginning) and the rim (end), symbolic elements of para-
mount importance in Japanese tea bowl aesthetics.[31] Despite its
generic "ice bucket" designation, this work more closely resembles
a crucible, cauldron, or volcanic crater with congealed lava form-
ing the progressive tiers and overflowing rim. Voulkos thus created
a form that appears to lack artifice or even intent, reflecting his
belief that "The ideal form is no ideal form. The clay and its colors
signify an endless potential and flow of information."[32]

Voulkos has perhaps come closest to achieving his ideal of "no
ideal form" through his "stack" sculptures. Revealing their debt to
the Abstract Expressionist and Zen Buddhist emphasis on process,
the stacks are named for the act of their creation, in which several
irregular cylindrical components are shaped, vertically stacked,
and fused together with clay and slip. These basic components,

often augmented with inclusions that resemble pebbles, bricks, or stones, are pushed, pulled, carved, slashed, and gouged, in an intensely physical process that recalls Jackson Pollock's "action painting," and that Voulkos has likened to dancing.[33] Weighing up to four hundred pounds and reaching heights of up to four feet, Voulkos's stacks continually test the creative capabilities of their creator and the physical limitations of his materials.

Like a Zen calligraphy exercise, Voulkos's focus on the stack—a single volumetric form that can be explored in all its physical and conceptual permutations—represents a conscious restriction of his formal means towards an amplification of his expressive ends. Unlike his plates and ice buckets, which gain much of their expressive power from their subversion of their ostensible, functional models, Voulkos's stacks lack any specific real-life counterpart or perceptible use, yet are characterized by an aura of primordial power.

The extraordinary range of chromatic effects that characterizes Voulko's stacks are the result of his emulation of comparable effects in Japanese ceramics and of his collaboration with Peter Callas, who has mastered the art of wood-firing ceramics. Modeled on ancient Japanese prototypes, Callas's room-size, semi-subterranean *anagama* (hole or tunnel kiln) consumes several cords of wood during weeklong firings that generate temperatures of up to 2,300 degrees Fahrenheit. While some of the surface effects associated with wood-firing can be induced by kiln placement, the type of wood fuel, and the duration of the firing, most of the determining factors remain beyond the artist's control. The *anagama* thus provided Voulkos with a means of emulating a fundamental aspect of the Zen ceramic tradition—the introduction of chance and accident into a process in which absolute control typically is prized.[34]

Like Voulkos's contemporaneous plates, *Untitled (Stack)* of 1980 (fig. 19; p. 136) reflects his interest in projecting his calligraphic and painterly concerns into three dimensions, but through a more complex interaction between surface and structural concerns. The painterly quality of this stack's smoky, wood-fired surface reveals

Voulkos's emulation of Japanese ceramics, but contrasts strongly with the raw sculptural physicality of the slashes and gouges. A subtle surface tension is created by the protruding ridges that gird each of the three stacked cylinders, suggesting that the clay has been stretched over an internal structural support, not unlike the reeds that support Japanese paper lamps. Treating this stack like a three-dimensional canvas, Voulkos has animated its surface with seemingly random gestural marks.

The long, arcing lines that penetrate the stack's surface skin to varying depths resemble incisions or scars, and act as visual counterpoints to the work's curved silhouette. The X-shaped intersections of these arcing lines are often marked by a circular puncture, suggestive of a point of collision or impact. The short, slightly curved gouges with rounded edges resemble paint strokes made by fingers or brushes, or perhaps the tubelike tracks found in weathered wood or fossilized stone. These gouges violate the physical integrity essential to functional ceramic vessels and enable the viewer to look into, through, and out of the stack form. Through this fluid interchangeability of form and space, Voulkos

Fig. 19. Peter Voulkos, *Untitled (Stack)*, 1980, stoneware, 46 × 15 in. diameter

Fig. 20. Peter Voulkos, *Yogi*, 1997, stoneware, 46 × 32 × 25 in.

integrates the interiors and exteriors of his stack sculptures into the surrounding environment.

Although Voulkos had violated the surface integrity of earlier sculptures, this aspect of his work was reinforced by his 1967 meeting with Lucio Fontana (1899–1968), an artist best known for his punctured and slashed canvases. Fontana's theory of "Spatialism" questioned the validity of traditional two-dimensional canvas and paper supports, and argued that artists should create works in the three physical dimensions, plus the fourth dimension of time, in order to redefine the surrounding environment. Fontana's interest in process, chance and accident, his radical manipulation of materials, and his desire to break down the barriers between painting and sculpture, as well as between nature and art, paralleled Voulkos's own interests. The power of Voulkos's early stacks is largely a function of their ability to hold these seemingly competing concerns—nature and art, painting and sculpture, surface and structure, subtlety and raw physicality—in a state of balanced tension.

One of Voulkos's most recent stacks, *Yogi* (fig. 20; p. 137) of 1997, reveals a complex interaction between the dualities of geology/landscape and architecture/cityscape. Voulkos has observed that his artistic aesthetic of emulating the forces and forms of nature was partly inspired by the geology of his native Montana: "It's the rock formations and the mountains of Montana, lots of layers. Everything is layered in nature. On a road, you see how the glaciers came through and pushed rocks up and out: layers of antiquity."[35] Voulkos's stacks, which may be seen as equivalents to nature's geological layering process, reveal his fascination with both the gradual and the catastrophic forces of nature. The hourglass profile of *Yogi* recalls the uneven erosion that occurs when a soft sedimentary sandstone is sandwiched between harder layers of stone. The extraordinary cleavage and near decapitation of *Yogi*'s upper third, which rests precariously cantilevered over its base, evokes the violent forces operative in nature.

The landscape associations of *Yogi* are accentuated by Voulkos's use of high-silica-content clay imported from Shigaraki, one of Japan's "Six Ancient Kilns," and by its wood-firing in Peter Callas's *anagama*, which was modeled on a traditional Shigaraki kiln. The combination of intense heat, smoke, and wood ash generated by this 2,300-degree inferno transformed *Yogi* into a substance that resembles weathered stone, unevenly covered with a natural glaze that exhibits extraordinary variations in its coloration, texture, and finish. Japanese tea ceremony aficionados often refer to the surface glazes and firing patterns of Shigaraki ware as its "scenery," comparable to that of a rock garden or a landscape painting.[36]

Yogi bears a particularly prized effect known as *koge* (scorch), which occurs when the firing process has completely oxidized the natural glaze, leaving a sooty, gray-black residue often likened by connoisseurs to moss on boulders.[37] This scorch effect, which is most visible around the neck of *Yogi*, heightens this sculpture's resemblance to an oven, kiln, or furnace topped by a smokestack. However, Voulkos has drawn a more revealing analogy between his stacks and natural infernos by naming *Stromboli* (1993) and *Pinatubo* (1994) after volcanoes. These titles are not intended to be interpreted literally, but rather metaphorically, with the stack's physical form symbolizing the primordial forces of creation.

Despite its outward resemblance to a seemingly random accretion of geological forms, *Yogi* also manifests a strong sense of underlying architectonic order. However, unlike *Untitled (Stack)* of 1980, which was shaped in a single organic act of creation, *Yogi* appears to have been constructed and reconstructed during several distinct and complex building campaigns. *Yogi*'s architectonic order is most apparent in the vertical and horizontal bricklike or stonelike inclusions in the stack surface—particularly in a sequence of four stepped stones that ascend the stack's circumference. More subtly, the sharp termination of *Yogi*'s rounded "shoulder" resembles the edges created as the smooth outer cladding of an ancient architectural form crumbles away over time to reveal the cruder support structure beneath. This phenomenon occurs most famously in Egypt's Great Pyramids, which Voulkos has conceptually linked to his architectonic stacks through the titles of his collage *Pyramid of the Sacrifice* (1984) and his stack *King's Chamber* (1992).[38]

However, this type of fragmentation and decay also characterizes the architectural ruins found in contemporary cities such as Berkeley and Oakland, where Voulkos has lived since 1959. While acknowledging the formative influence of the Montana landscape and its geological formations on his work, Voulkos also has drawn inspiration from this urban landscape: "Give me the dirt, grime, and graffiti of the city. I like the nervousness and tension of urban life, and I use them."[39] Drawing an analogy between the ruins of the past and those of the present, Voulkos emphasizes the transient nature of both the natural and built environments.

In addition to their overt references to geological or architectural forms, Voulkos's stacks also resonate with anthropomorphic associations. His stacks have been compared to both the technique and form of fourth- to seventh-century Japanese *haniwa*, grave guardian figures, which are constructed of unglazed, stacked cylinders and slabs.[40] A further comparison might be made with the large eighth-century B.C. Geometric vessels used as grave markers in the Kerameikos Cemetery located in the potters' quarter in Athens. These markers, which include five-foot-tall, ovoid amphorae with tall columnar necks, may have been used as offering vessels for funerary rituals.[41]

Rather than replicating the physical forms of these historical antecedents, Voulkos's stacks share their symbolic function as human surrogates and as mediators between matter and spirit. As in the Great Pyramids that have inspired Voulkos, this mediating function is expressed through the stack form, which is anchored to the earth through a flared base and rises upwards toward the heavens. Voulkos explicitly rendered this metaphysical relationship in his collage *Pyramid of the Amphora* (1985), in which the architectonic forms of the Egyptian pyramid and the Greek amphora are fused and augmented by starlike pushpins and a steep staircase that ascends the outside of the form. Voulkos's anthropomorphic title, *Yogi*, affirms the human presence that emanates from this work, as well as the eternal human yearning for mystical and spiritual enlightenment.

ROBERT ARNESON—FACING REALITY

During a career that spanned three decades, Robert Arneson played an influential role in reintroducing into American art real (often prosaic) subject matter, strong social content and commentary, and overt emotion (especially satirical humor), all of which had been devalued by mainstream modernism's emphasis on formal issues. Naturally resistant to artificial and restrictive classifications, and dissatisfied with the art world's reluctant and condescending recognition of ceramics as a separate (but not quite equal) means of artistic expression, Arneson used his marginalized medium to challenge and critique many of the contemporary art world's beliefs and values. Fusing a strong editorial stance with extraordinary technical innovations, Arneson produced a body of unconventional work that, as Peter Voulkos observed, "just annihilated and destroyed concepts people had about clay."[42]

A major turning point in Arneson's early career occurred in 1961 at the Sacramento State Fair, where he threw a simple demonstration pot that unintentionally resembled a quart-size bottle of beer and spontaneously decided to seal it with a clay cap and label it "NO DEPOSIT, NO RETURN." Arneson's self-conscious gesture marked a conceptual and physical break with the ceramic tradition of functional vessels and may be viewed as a manifestation of the artist's observation that "the whole California ceramics thing basically started as an iconoclastic nose-thumbing at the art establishment."[43] Pioneering the movement that became known as California Funk, Arneson subsequently created ceramic objects characterized by their intensely handworked and vividly painted surfaces, expressive emotionalism, and an inclination to anthropomorphism, all of which served an intensely personal artistic vision that inevitably led him to self-portraiture.

Arneson overtly tackled the subject of three-dimensional self-portraiture with a second pivotal work, the *Self-Portrait of the Artist Losing His Marbles* (1965).[44] Arneson had begun this work as a relatively conventional portrait bust, but it had cracked from the head to the base after numerous firings. By inserting glass marbles into the crack and giving the work its humorous, self-deprecating title, Arneson acknowledged the uncharacteristic artificiality of his original intention and also reaffirmed his commitment to the systematic deconstruction of ceramic conventions. Although Arneson did not create another major self-portrait for six years, *Self-Portrait of the Artist Losing His Marbles* openly acknowledged the artist's symbiotic relationship with his work. When Arneson returned to self-portraiture in 1971, he created a remarkable series of heads, including *A Hollow Jesture* (fig. 21; p. 187), in which he explored the molding of personal and artistic identity.

In retrospect, Arneson's embrace of portraiture, the bust format, and a naturalistic style reinvigorated artistic conventions that supposedly had been rendered irrelevant by mainstream modernism. However, these works also pierced the formal pretensions of the traditional portrait bust through their provocative subject matter and their subversion of sculptural conventions. Arneson's transposition of crude earthenware for the more permanent media of marble or bronze implicitly devalued these materials and introduced an earthy *vanitas* theme. His extensive use of colored glazes also challenged portrait bust conventions, despite the fact that equally vivid colors had been applied to many ancient sculptures. Finally, by omitting a traditional base from most of these works, Arneson not only suggested that his own work should not be placed "on a pedestal," but that he had taken traditional sculpture down off its pedestal and reintegrated it with real life.

Arneson's early self-portraits owe a clear debt to caricaturists such as William Hogarth (1697–1764) and Honoré Daumier (1808–1879), who exaggerated or distorted human anatomy in the pursuit of penetrating psychological portraits of human nature. Arneson also cited as a source of inspiration the "psychotic self-portraits screaming and grimacing" created by the Austrian sculptor Frances Xavier Messerschmidt (1736–1783).[45] An undated Arneson notebook sketch copied after the *Self-Portrait with a Funny Face* by the Flemish artist Adriaen Brouwer (1605–1638) provided the inspiration for Arneson's first self-portrait mask *Exaggeration* (1972) and reveals his interest in the baroque conceit of depicting extreme expressions and emotions as the primary subject of an artwork.[46]

Perhaps the most relevant precedent for Arneson's gallery of self-portraits, however, was provided by the most famous practitioner of this subject, Rembrandt van Rijn (1606–1669), whose *Self-Portrait Open Mouthed, as if Shouting* (fig. 22) shares Brouwer's interest in capturing a vivid, lifelike likeness. Hidden beneath the surface appearances of both Rembrandt's and Arneson's more theatrical performances, however, is a deep fascination with, and understanding of, the virtues, vices, and

Fig. 21. Robert Arneson, *A Hollow Jesture*, 1971, glazed earthenware, 20¼ × 12½ × 14 in.

Fig. 22. Rembrandt van Rijn (1606–1669), *Self-Portrait Open Mouthed, as if Shouting: Bust,* 1630, etching, 2¾ × 2⅜ in., Fine Arts Museums of San Francisco, Achenbach Foundation for Graphic Arts, Bruno and Sadie Adriani Collection, 1959.40.3

vicissitudes of the human condition. Although Rembrandt's youthful hubris exerted the strongest influence on Arneson's early self-portraits, the Dutch artist's extraordinary artistic passage to middle-age reflection and old-age introspection, tempered by experience and mortality, had increasing resonance for Arneson.

In *A Hollow Jesture,* created a decade after Arneson's breakthrough *No Deposit, No Return* (1961), the artist looks in the mirror and unflinchingly records the physical and psychic toll exacted by a decade as an art world iconoclast. In an unidealized, almost clinical self-examination, Arneson meticulously catalogues the visible signs of middle-aged mortality—the scars and wrinkles etched in his face, the receding hairline and snowy white beard, and the large hearing aid required by his hereditary hearing loss, a constant reminder of human imperfection. The yellow, almost jaundiced cast of the face, suggestive of an inner buildup of bile, offers a tongue-in-cheek portrayal of Arneson's self-acknowledged reputation as an irascible art world malcontent: "I weigh 182 lbs. I'm 5'8" tall, I wear hearing aids in each ear, strain to hear but seldom understand significant issues, causing acute paranoia and irritableness. Liquor helps—clay recommended for therapy."[47]

In the defining and defiant action of *A Hollow Jesture,* Arneson sticks out his tongue at the viewer. This startling gesture, often used by baroque artists as an allegory for "taste" in their depictions of the five senses, here is transformed by Arneson into a punning exercise in "bad taste," and a visual embodiment of his artistic philosophy: "I want to make 'high' art that is outrageous, while revealing the human condition which is not always so high."[48] While Arneson's gesture may be viewed within a broader cultural context of late 1960s–early 1970s social and political nonconformity (a seemingly irrational gesture as a response to irrational times), it also embodies Arneson's convention-flaunting approach to art and life. Extracted from everyday life, permanently memorialized in sculptural form, and elevated to the realm of high art, Arneson's confrontational gesture serves as a permanent challenge to the conventional viewer or critic.

Implicit in Arneson's extended series of self-portraits, however, is the distinction between portraiture and caricature, and between our inner identity and the mask that we present to the world. Like its baroque precedents, *A Hollow Jesture* appears to depict authentic, raw, human emotion, yet is in actuality the product of an intellectual conceit. Ostensibly embodying a sincere and defiant artistic stance, Arneson's self-portrait also may be viewed as a self-conscious caricature of his public persona as the "bad boy" of the art world. Despite the aura of authenticity that accrues to many of Arneson's unidealized self-portraits, attempts to interpret them as unadulterated equivalents for the artist are complicated by his revelation that "I never did a self-portrait. I always use a self-portrait as a mask."[49]

Arneson's punning title identifies the self-portrait mask in *A Hollow Jesture* as that of a jester, a professional fool or buffoon who provided jests or amusements for royal courts and noble households during the Middle Ages and the Renaissance. Like a caricaturist, the jester's ostensible purpose was to provide entertainment, but his true purpose was to draw attention to human foibles and failings through the use of satire. Permitted by convention to transgress societal norms, the jester was empowered to say what no one else could or would say to individuals occupying positions of political and/or social power. Arneson's appropriation of the jester's identity overtly acknowledges his perception of the artist's important role as a social critic, one who utilizes humor as a potent weapon to combat hypocrisy. In his role as an iconoclast and provocateur, Arneson transgressed both artistic and societal conventions, and implicitly gave his viewers license to do the same.

Arneson's humorous social satire often conflicted with art-world pretentiousness, and subjected him to criticisms that he was not a "serious" artist, but rather the humorous "class clown" of the ceramic world—an identity he parodied in *Klown* (1978). Rejecting both the mainstream art world's standards and this one-dimensional stereotype, Arneson argued for a redefinition of terms: "The things that I'm really interested in as an artist are the things you can't do—and that's mix humor and fine art. I'm not being silly about it, I'm serious about the combination. Humor is generally considered low art but I think humor is very serious— it points out the fallacies of our existence."[50]

As an artistic response to his critics, *A Hollow Jesture* parodies critical resistance to ceramics as a serious art form by subverting their stereotype as purely functional vessel forms lacking serious content. The dark, hollow void visible behind Arneson's absent eyes plays on criticisms of California artists in general, and Arneson in particular, as intellectually shallow and empty-headed, a motif and theme that was revisited in one of the artist's most famous works, *California Artist* (1982).[51] Like the ridiculous head that typically crowned the medieval jester's staff, Arneson's violently distorted facial expression and bulging neck tendons convey the visual impression of an actual head that has been sharply severed at the base of the neck, perhaps by the artist's critics, whom he greets with one last, defiant gesture.

STEPHEN DE STAEBLER—MATTER INTO SPIRIT

Stephen De Staebler studied art, art history, and religion at Princeton University, painting at Black Mountain College, North Carolina, with Ben Shahn and Robert Motherwell, and sculpture at the University of California, Berkeley. His sculptural work was transformed by his study with Peter Voulkos, who emphasized the organic qualities of clay, the potential of large-scale ceramic sculpture, and the total fusion of the artist with his work. Embracing and extending Voulkos's aesthetic, De Staebler replicated the forces of chaos and order that he perceived in nature, and employed gravity and the force of his own body to endow clay with an expressive physicality that was tempered by an underlying structure.

In the 1960s, De Staebler created landscape sculptures characterized by a radical horizontality at odds with the vertical aspirations of traditional sculptural monuments. Resembling natural geological formations shaped by cataclysmic events and weathered by erosion, these organic clay reliefs do not appear to have been constructed by human hands, but rather merely discovered or excavated. Describing his fascination with the primordial power of clay, De Staebler has observed, "It had this great power to receive order, but also to persist in its randomness. In that sense, it's landscape, because landscape itself is randomness being acted upon by overwhelming forces, which have only recently been discovered or understood. You think of earth crust movement, plate tectonics, and so forth."[52] De Staebler was able to replicate these larger geological forces through his innovative use of smaller component parts that were fired individually and then fitted together into larger, continuous wholes.

By the 1970s, the nascent anthropomorphic element of De Staebler's early landscape sculptures had evolved into free-standing, monolithic figures embodying concepts of geology, history, and archaeology. *Pointing Figure Column* (fig. 23; p. 167) of 1985 resembles the remains of an ancient sculpture that was carved from a quarried block of striated sandstone, and then weathered by the elements over centuries. This geological aspect of both De Staebler's landscape and figural works may be traced to childhood memories of a river near his family's Indiana farm that was "bordered by a sandstone bluff intricately carved by water and wind. It had caves and natural stairways up fissures just wide enough to squeeze through. I sometimes think that my impulses were all formed as a child there."[53]

Both modeled from, and supported by, the primordial medium of clay, *Pointing Figure Column* incorporates the remnants of a

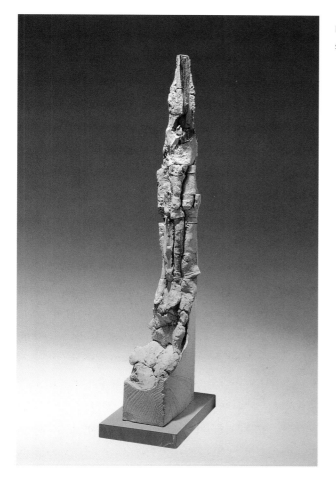

Fig. 23. Stephen De Staebler, *Pointing Figure Column*, 1985, stoneware, porcelain, and oxides, 96 × 15¼ × 21 in.

architectonic, and archaeological associations with greater permanence. Similarly, the featureless figure's weathered surface is marred by cracks, breaks, and fissures that simultaneously suggest both decomposition and permanent petrification. These qualities have prompted comparisons of similar De Staebler works with ancient figural artworks, including the Egyptian temple of Ramses II at Abu Simbel (ca. 1257 b.c.), Cycladic idols (ca. 2500–1100 b.c.), and Greek Kouros/Kore figures (6th–7th centuries b.c.).

De Staebler has likened the construction of his human figures from component parts to the modernist techniques of collage and assemblage, "where you take fragments that speak to one another and bring them into some kind of field that is more than the sum of its parts."[54] De Staebler replicates this process when he creates new works through a process that he has termed "spontaneous archaeology"—the recycling and reassembling of sculpture fragments that have been buried or deposited in the hill and "boneyard" behind his Berkeley studio.[55]

The power of De Staebler's figures is partially predicated on the tension created between their potential fragmentation or fusion. Commenting upon the disturbing visual dismemberment of his figures, De Staebler has observed that "The expression of physical loss in a figure has power because it makes us aware of our incompleteness."[56] De Staebler's fragmentary figures thus are evocative of modern existential experience, in which the solitary individual feels physically, psychically, or spiritually alienated from contemporary society. However, De Staebler's figures, embedded in their earthly cradles, also embody the instinctual human desire to recover and to reconnect with a meaningful past and a collective humanity. Similarly, the physical dissolution of the figures may be interpreted as a metaphor for the immersion of human existence within a larger being or godhead.

Because they incorporate these references to antiquity, De Staebler's stelalike works are often perceived as having commemorative or funerary associations. However, De Staebler maintains an important distinction between the antique and the archaic. While

fragmentary human figure whose physical and metaphysical attributes are progressively transformed from its base to its apex. The base (and perhaps portions of the figure itself) appear to have eroded and slumped away beneath the figure's feet, leaving them suspended in midair. The recognizable, relatively intact lower legs and feet contrast with the upper portions of the legs, which resemble decaying flesh and weathered bone, and with the upper portion of the figure, which resembles a single, hollow cross section of a scorched human bone or spinal column. In the defining gesture of the work, the downward-pointing feet suggest both the pull of gravity on the dead weight of the corporeal body, as well as the liberation of the body from the earthly realm as it rises upwards. This progression from solid rock to hollow voids, and from flesh into bone, may be viewed as a metaphor for the transformation of matter into spirit.

While the skeletal appearance of *Pointing Figure Column* evokes associations with human mortality, its frontality and fusion with the stacked, stonelike support blocks also encourage geologic, the antique conjures up images of archaeology and art history, the archaic evokes timeless archetypes of mythic and spiritual belief. Thus, the apparent erosion of the figure may be seen, not simply as an excavation of its underlying skeletal corporeality, but rather as a revelation of its inner spirit.

It is also possible to view the figure as simultaneously materializing out of, or dissolving into, its earthly medium. These dualities reflect De Staebler's belief that "The obsessive quality of art is an attempt to reconcile opposites and keep an equilibrium. If you strip away the dogmas and doctrines, religion becomes a very precarious relationship between a frail and finite reality and a sense of all-present infinite reality."[57] De Staebler's *Pointing Figure Column* embodies the duality of the human existence, which acknowledges the realities of earthbound materiality and mortality, but also aspires to transcendent and immortal spirituality.

JOHN CEDERQUIST—AGAINST THE GRAIN

John Cederquist's innovative wood constructions, which blur the distinctions between furniture, sculpture, and painting, have challenged and deconstructed almost every preconception of traditional furniture craftsmanship.[58] Drawing from art history and popular culture sources as diverse as nineteenth-century Japanese color woodcuts and twentieth-century Popeye cartoons, Cederquist has created works that expand the boundaries between two and three dimensions, illusion and reality, image and object. Like other artists of his generation, Cederquist has referred to the issue of functionality—the standard measure of a successful piece of modernist furniture—as "always a gray area" in his work.[59] He also has observed that the modernist mantra "form follows function" does not take into account the primacy of his images, which ultimately constitute the most important "function" of his furniture.[60]

Cederquist's desire to explore the boundaries between two- and three-dimensional representation has been facilitated by his innovative use of solid wood veneers laminated onto plywood. Historically, wood veneer has been used by furniture craftsmen for a variety of reasons, including aesthetic preference, necessity (when the desired wood was not strong enough to serve a struc-

tural function), and cost (when the desired wood was too rare or expensive to use in quantity). Wood veneer often functions as an implicit form of trompe l'oeil, by creating the illusion that the two-dimensional wood surface continues into the three-dimensional substructure of the furniture. Wood veneer marquetry also has been used to create trompe l'oeil scenes or objects that fuse pictorial and spatial illusion, most notably in Renaissance and baroque furniture and architectural interiors.

Like the viewers of trompe l'oeil paintings, the viewers of Cederquist's work are rarely, if ever, completely "fooled." Indeed, Cederquist often violates a central tenet of trompe l'oeil art—that the artist not depict animate objects or elements that will betray the pictorial illusion by their immobility. In addition, much of the visual and emotional impact (and pleasure) of trompe l'oeil works is derived from the realization that the artist is attempting to fool the viewer—and that these works require the viewer's willing suspension of disbelief for the illusion to succeed.

This symbiotic relationship between pictorial illusionism and the viewer's reciprocal vision also is a characteristic of Western linear perspective. However, this Renaissance-derived method of viewing the world around us (and artistic representations of it) is so ingrained in our senses that we are no longer capable of seeing linear perspective as a method or "frame of reference" at all—rather, it appears to us as part of the natural order.

Cederquist challenges this "natural" order through his manipulative use of fixed-point perspective, which establishes a single ideal viewing position for his works. The slightest deviation from this ideal position reveals that Cederquist's convincing illusions are the result of startling, even disturbing, distortions, which compel the viewer to return to the "proper" perspective position. Cederquist also subverts traditional linear perspective by utilizing it simultaneously with the isometric perspective employed in many forms of Asian art. In this perspectival system, lines and objects closest to the viewer appear to converge, while distance is conveyed by placing objects higher on the picture plane. By utilizing Asian isometric perspective in his work, Cederquist is able to reintroduce both a heightened awareness of the artificiality of perspectival systems and the sense of wonder that accompanies the viewer's recognition of such visual feats.

Like much of Cederquist's work, the origins of *Steamer Chest II* (fig. 24; p. 193) may be traced to his fascination with American cartoons of the 1940s and 1950s. Cederquist was especially fascinated by the cartoon artists' expressive use of minimal black, white, and gray lines and shading to convey three-dimensional forms and movement, the overlapping stage flats and scrims to create depth, and the unusual camera angles to create or to exaggerate perspective. Like the Hollywood cartoonists who calculated the degree of detail necessary within a single cel, or the number of cartoon cels required per second of film, Cederquist also confronted a question central to the creation of trompe l'oeil: how much visual information is necessary to create a credible illusion that does not dissolve into its constituent parts?

On a more practical level, Cederquist was struck by "a new genre of furniture in the cartoons, much more fluid, much more alive. I'm trying to figure out how I can exist in two worlds, how I can make this work in two worlds."[61] In homage to this parallel cartoon world, Cederquist created *Olive's Chair* (1982), which replicated Olive Oyl's chair in a Popeye cartoon. Cederquist's great revelation and innovation was to project this two-dimensional

cartoon object into a three-dimensional reality, while still retaining the fourth dimension of time implicit in the animated chair's perspectival distortions.[62] *Olive's Chair* and subsequent works, part drawn, part sculptural, and only marginally functional, have been evocatively described by Cederquist as existing in "two-and-a-half dimensions."[63]

The facade of Cederquist's *Steamer Chest II* is dominated by a single spiraling metal pipe that spews steam from its two open ends, two seams, and a puncture, causing the attached pressure gauge needle to fall. This steampipe, which lacks both a visible source and a purpose, is intertwined with a series of randomly stacked vertical wooden boards, only one of which (at the lower left) serves a visible support function for the pipe. Both the heavy metal steampipe and the wooden boards alternately appear to defy gravity, or to be in the process of collapsing. *Steamer Chest II* thus embodies a series of conceptual and pictorial contrasts—including those between order and disorder, containment and escape, solid pipes and amorphous steam, and progressively spiraling pipe and randomly piled boards.

Although a chest of drawers is one of the most traditional and functional furniture forms, *Steamer Chest II* lacks any visible drawers (although it has five) or drawer pulls, and is essentially unrecognizable as furniture by conventional standards. Particularly extraordinary is the disjunction between the beautifully rendered architectonic facade and the pedestrian plywood chest of drawers that supports it, a disjunction almost as radical as the difference between a painted canvas and its wooden stretcher bars. The fictive wooden boards, which could theoretically be used to construct a "real" steamer chest, are depicted merely as raw materials. A subtle reference to the architectonic crests and finials of eighteenth-century high chests, conveyed by the nearly symmetrical arrangement of boards that ascend toward the top, is subsumed by the kinetic jumble of pipe and planks.[64]

Steamer Chest II was preceded by an earlier series of small, wall-mounted cabinets that were inspired by the industrial refineries of

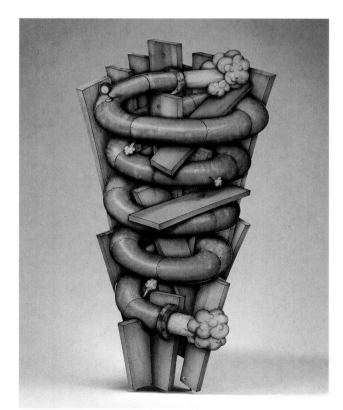

Fig. 24. John Cederquist, *Steamer Chest II*, 1994, Baltic birch plywood, ripple maple, poplar, epoxy resin, and lithography inks, 70¼ × 38 × 14⅝ in.

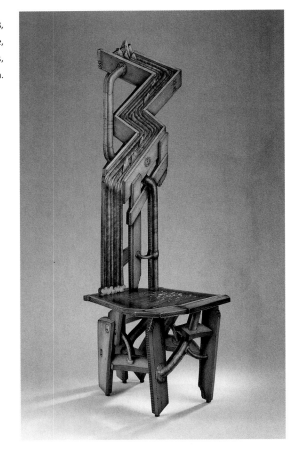

Fig. 25. John Cederquist, *Conservation Chair,* 1998,
Baltic birch plywood, Sitka spruce, maple,
epoxy resin, aniline dye, and lithography inks,
60½ × 19¾ × 24⅝ in.

Long Beach, California, and their "steam, smoke, and thousands of tubes going everywhere . . . there was always something venting off steam or a big flame."[65] Given Cederquist's self-description as the stereotypical Southern California "laid-back surfer," and his fondness for verbal and visual puns, it is also tempting to read personal associations into his use of "boards" (i.e., surfboards) and "tubular" "pipeline" (surfer jargon for ideal waves) in *Steamer Chest II.* Cederquist made this connection explicit in *Tubular* (1990), in which he paid artistic homage to every surfer's dream wave—the Japanese artist Katsushika Hokusai's *Great Wave at Kanagawa*—the most famous woodcut from a series entitled *Thirty-six Views of Mount Fuji* (ca. 1829–33).[66]

Cederquist's title "Steamer Chest" evokes images of "steamer trunks"—horizontal wood-frame chests designed to fit under the bunk beds of steamship passenger cabins. This association in turn evokes the historical age of steam, which fueled the locomotives, steamships, and factories of the Industrial Revolution. Cederquist's rendition of a humorous and harmless steampipe recalls a more innocent age that does not exist in reality, but lives on in cartoons. This source of artistic inspiration is clearly acknowledged by the schematic puffs of steam, which recall those emanating from Popeye's combination pipe/steamwhistle. Like its cartoon counterparts, *Steamer Chest II* is an ostensibly inanimate object magically brought to life, its "chest" expanding upwards from its "feet" in an anthropomorphic act of "hot air" exuberance or hubris. The appeal of the simple steam-driven devices that powered cartoon contraptions is considerable for contemporary viewers, who are increasingly reminded of the double-edged benefits and dangers of modern technology.

Cederquist's work also has been greatly influenced by Japanese ukiyo-e (pictures of the floating world)—color woodcuts produced during the Edo period (1615–1868). These prints, whose pictorial innovations transformed nineteenth-century European and American art, synthesized Chinese and Japanese landscape traditions with Asian isometric and Western linear perspective to create a new cross-cultural vision of the world. Although the works of the ukiyo-e masters Katsushika Hokusai (1760–1849) and Utagawa Hiroshige (1797–1858) have been elevated to fine art status, ukiyo-e originally represented an inexpensive form of popular and vernacular culture that informally depicted the lives of ordinary people. In addition to their populist appeal (and occasional humor), ukiyo-e share several similarities with cartoons, including the use of black contour lines to delineate form and to suggest volume, modeling, and movement; large flat fields of solid or shaded color; and radical croppings and extreme close-ups to create the illusion of depth behind the foreground forms.

Cederquist's acknowledged debt to Japanese ukiyo-e is manifested structurally, pictorially, and thematically in *Conservation Chair* (fig. 25; p. 192), which depicts water flowing past sharp rocks, down and over the edge of a wooden sluice, and into a trapezoidal collecting pool supported by wooden boards. The attenuated proportions of *Conservation Chair,* while reminiscent of early modernist chairs by Frank Lloyd Wright and Charles Rennie Mackintosh, also recall the verticality of Chinese and Japanese scroll paintings, as well as the *chū-tanzaku* format of ukiyo-e. Cederquist's use of Prussian blue recalls the widespread use of this distinctive color in ukiyo-e, especially those of Hokusai and Hiroshige. Imported from Europe into Japan in the early nineteenth century, this artificial pigment was highly valued for its desirable pictorial qualities of translucence and tinting strength. Prussian blue was often used in conjunction with *bokashi*, a printing technique for large areas of sky or water that achieved subtle illusionistic gradations from dark to light, similar to those in *Conservation Chair*.[67]

Close parallels to Cederquist's depiction of water in *Conservation Chair* may be observed in Hokusai's landscape series *A Tour of Japanese Waterfalls* (ca. 1833–34), whose prints are characterized by tightly cropped vertical compositions, providing dramatic examples of isometric perspective. Hokusai's waterfalls, some real and some imagined or exaggerated, are depicted as dynamic entities that are animated externally by their expressive silhouettes and internally by their stylized patterns of waves, ripples, and bubbles. The dynamic zigzag pattern of water coursing down the mountain in *The Waterfall at Yoshino Where Yoshitsune Washed His Horse* (fig. 26) recalls the similar compositional device in

Fig. 26. Katsushika Hokusai (1760–1849), *The Waterfall at Yoshino Where Yoshitsune Washed His Horse,* from *A Tour of Japanese Waterfalls,* ca. 1833–34, color woodcut, 14½ × 9⁵⁄₁₆ in., Fine Arts Museums of San Francisco, Achenbach Foundation for Graphic Arts, 1963.30.20336.

Conservation Chair, as do the straight, vertical drops of waterfalls over a precipice in two other prints from the series—*The Falls at Ono on the Kiso Road* and *Yoro Waterfall in Mino Province.*[68]

Hokusai's prints are perhaps less important as pictorial sources for Cederquist's *Conservation Chair* than as models of Japanese attitudes towards nature and its conservation. His prints reveal the necessity of maintaining a delicate balance between nature and culture in a small country with limited natural resources and a high population density. In particular, the prevalence of water as a ukiyo-e motif reflects this element's importance for an island nation whose economy and culture are dependent upon maritime trade, as well as upon water-based food staples such as rice and fish. In Hokusai's print *Waterwheel at Onden,* from the series *Thirty-six Views of Mount Fuji,* a river is temporarily diverted to power a rice mill waterwheel, and then is channeled away through a wooden sluice resembling the one in *Conservation Chair.*[69]

This small-scale husbanding of water in nineteenth-century Japan offers a sharp contrast with the nearly contemporaneous use of hydraulic mining and wooden sluices during the American Gold Rush era, techniques that left permanent scars on the American landscape. Wasteful and destructive water practices continue today in the massive flooding employed to irrigate agricultural fields, as well as in the draining of lakes, rivers, and natural aquifers to supply new real estate developments—phenomena that are particularly prevalent in Cederquist's native Southern California.

Cederquist's *Conservation Chair* is one of a series of works in which he has explored the conservation theme through depictions of water, flowing through wooden sluices and pools that hold trees and fish. The series was inspired in part by news reports that salmon swimming upstream to spawn in the American Northwest were unable to use the fish ladders constructed to help them bypass hydraulic dams.[70] Our problematic impact on the environment is expressed in *Conservation Chair* through a contrast

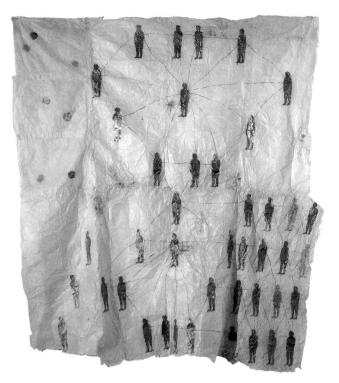

Fig. 27. Kiki Smith, *Untitled*, 1993, silkscreen, ink, and gold leaf on Nepal paper and Thai tissue, 75 × 80 in.

between free-flowing water and its containment, and between handmade wooden sluices and machine-made pipes. However, the potential preservation of natural resources is also suggested by the large metal pipe, which appears to recycle the water from the collecting pool back to the top of the wooden sluice, which bears a Japanese calligraphic inscription reading "conservation."

Given Cederquist's acknowledged artistic debt to Japanese prints, it is worth recalling that the word *ukiyo-e* is derived from *ukiyo*, a Buddhist word that refers to the transient and illusory nature of life on earth.[71] This theme was implicit in Hokusai's series, *Thirty-Six Views of Mount Fuji*, in which the ancient and immovable mountain was contrasted with the temporal lives and endeavors of the people living in the surrounding landscape. Through a confluence of Japanese and American cultural concerns in *Conservation Chair*, Cederquist suggests that the respect accorded to nature in nineteenth-century ukiyo-e prints might provide a workable model for the harmonious coexistence of nature and culture in contemporary society.

KIKI SMITH: THE BODY POLITIC

Although Kiki Smith's mother, opera singer Jane Wilson, and her father, protominimalist sculptor Tony Smith, provided artistic role models, Smith did not define her own identity as an artist until the age of twenty-four, observing, "I always liked making things, but I liked crafts more than art."[72] Smith's own artistic sensibility was influenced less by the geometric minimalism of her father's monumental metal sculptures than by the fragile paper, wood, canvas, and wire works created by artist Richard Tuttle, a family friend who had assisted with the fabrication of her father's sculptures.[73] These influences helped to shape Smith's later work, which incorporates natural and/or handmade materials such as glass, ceramic, fiber, beads, beeswax, and human hair, bridging the arbitrary boundaries between art and craft, as well as the gender stereotypes historically associated with media such as fiber.

Synthesizing elements of realism, neoexpressionism, and conceptualism, Smith's work is distinguished by its ongoing emphasis on the human body as a site of artistic exploration, as well as of social, cultural, and political engagement. Drawing inspiration from pioneering women artists such as Louise Bourgeois, Eva Hesse, and Nancy Spero, and from male artists such as Joseph Beuys and Bruce Nauman, Smith has created provocative, visceral investigations of the human body, its external and internal organs, and their functions and fluids. Through her emotionally evocative and intellectually articulate use of the human figure, Smith has helped to reestablish the human body as a viable subject for contemporary artists. Smith's feminist sensibility also has led her to confront complex stereotypes and taboos associated with historical and contemporary perceptions of the female body, particularly those that have fostered the societal marginalization of women.

Images of forty-two diminutive, androgynous, and featureless human figures populate Smith's wall-mounted, curtainlike *Untitled* of 1993 (fig. 27; p. 230), whose large scale is mediated by its creation from smaller pieces of delicate, irregular, handmade and hand-joined paper. The simplified silhouettes of the human figures recall the flat dolls Smith made and sold during her early years as an artist in New York City. The human subject of *Untitled* is echoed by the work's supple, translucent, and luminous tissue paper support, which Smith has used in several works for its analogies to the human body's "envelope" of skin.[74] *Flower Blanket* (1994), for example, replicates on another pieced-paper sheet "the average surface of the human body unfolded, cut up, and laid flat in a grid."[75] These works were inspired in part by a newspaper article that described human skin, not as a solid barrier between internal organs and the external environment, but as a permeable tissue membrane—a revelation with particular resonance for Smith, whose works often accentuate the physical and psychological vulnerability of the human body.[76]

In contrast to the nearly identical and anonymous human figures, the surface of *Untitled* is also imprinted with several life-size images of eyes and lips that resemble rubbings made directly from the artist's own face and skin. This intensely personal, even intimate, revelation of Smith's own body and identity was prefigured shortly before *Untitled* in her monumental twelve-part lithograph entitled *Banshee Pearls* (1991), which incorporated the first recognizable images of the artist's face.[77] Smith's self-portraits on the "skin" of *Untitled* also recall Jasper Johns's *Study for Skin I–IV* (1962), in which Johns pressed his oil-coated face and hands against sheets of paper that were then dusted with powdered graphite to reveal the resulting self-portraits.[78] Both Smith's and Johns's self-portraits may be viewed as metaphors for the two artists' intense self-identification with their works, as well as the degree to which they are imprisoned by their reluctance to reveal too much of themselves or their emotions to the viewer.

Raised as a Catholic and deeply influenced by Christian theology (particularly Thomas Aquinas) and religious art (especially Matthias Grunewald's *Isenheim Altarpiece* of 1512–16), Smith has inflected much of her art with religious associations.[79] The presence of the fragmentary eyes and lips in *Untitled* recalls the *milagro* tradition, in which stamped-tin ex-voto offerings representing individual body parts are placed with religious images to request or acknowledge the healing of those parts by divine intervention. The white, clothlike paper itself recalls religious relics such as the Shroud of Turin or Veronica's Veil, fabrics imprinted with the ghostly images of Christ's body and face. Smith's transposition of the simplified silhouettes of anonymous human figures to

the recognizable, iconic image of a religious figure reflects her personal belief that ordinary human beings and their bodies deserve the same respect and reverence as religious icons and their relics.

Perhaps the most striking compositional element of *Untitled* is Smith's linking of almost all of the human figures with painted red lines that resemble the bloodlines of genealogical tables or family trees. This motif has art-historical precedents ranging from ancient Mesoamerican genealogical records to the Spanish Colonial *lienzo*, a large fabric sheet constructed from pieced cotton panels, but also incorporates pictographic glyphs and textual glosses that convey genealogical, cartographic, and historical information.[80] A more recent incarnation of these pictorial precedents occurs in the works of a feminist icon much admired by Smith—Mexican artist Frida Kahlo—who used bloodlines and veins in her paintings to suggest psychological and emotional (as well as biological) linkages.

The implicit presence of genetic lineage in *Untitled* is confirmed by its explicit depiction in her earlier work *Lucy's Daughters* (1991).[81] Both works share the pieced-paper format, and both are covered with groups of humanoid figures that are visibly linked. In *Lucy's Daughters*, the connections are clearly biological; white fiber strings connect the umbilicus and womb of the solitary female figure at the bottom of the work to an exponentially widening group of women and fetuses above. These women are the direct descendants of "Lucy," whose name identifies her with the recently discovered three-million-year-old Ethiopian hominid skeleton.[82] Lucy's remains not only provided a "missing link" in the human genealogical and evolutionary puzzle, but also raised provocative sociopolitical issues concerning gender (who was the first woman or "Eve"?) and race (are all humans descended from Africans?).

Unlike the relatively traditional genealogical tree depicted in *Lucy's Daughters*, the linked figures in *Untitled* are arranged within more complex kinship systems, in which individual figures may be viewed simultaneously as parents, progeny, and siblings. Although the hexagonal group at the top of the sheet clearly springs from a central figure, the more complex interconnections between the figures below and to the right render it impossible to assign primacy to any one individual or group. This visualization of the complexities of human relations may reflect alternate anthropological theories and discoveries regarding the possibility of multiple human origins. However, it also is consistent with Smith's statement that she focuses on the human body because "it's something everyone shares, and there is no hierarchy; it doesn't distinguish between class or race."[83] Unlike the human bodies in *Lucy's Daughters*, those in *Untitled* are neither female nor male, suggesting an evolution from gender-based concerns to a more encompassing and inclusive view of humanity.

Through its physical construction and thematic message, *Untitled* manifests Smith's ongoing fascination with issues of individual and collective human identity. While the human figures have been duplicated from a single archetype, thus utilizing artistic replication as a metaphor for biological reproduction, they are differentiated by their slightly irregular underlying yellow auras and overlays of metal leaf. These simultaneously identical and yet unique figures function as symbols for our own duality as genetically linked, yet psychologically differentiated, individuals. The three figures at the far left, who lack the animating yellow halos of their counterparts, are perhaps less emblematic of a genealogical or evolutionary dead end than of the isolated state of human beings who do not acknowledge and embrace their collective humanity.

Like its physical creation from component sheets, Smith's *Untitled* supports an interconnected humanity that is larger than the sum of its parts, and thus encourages viewers to assume responsibility for the care and preservation of our extended human family. As Smith has observed, "our bodies have been broken apart bit by bit and need a lot of healing; our whole society is very fragmented. . . . Everything is split, and presented as dichotomies—male/female, body/mind—and those splits need mending."[84] This is one of the defining themes of Smith's career, where individual works often focus on personal issues of physical and psychological fragmentation, but whose larger body of work provides a remarkably consistent and redemptive affirmation of universal humanity.

CRAFT INTO CONTENT

Kiki Smith is representative of a growing number of artists who perceive their choice and use of multiple media as the formal means to an expressive end, not as an affirmation of art or craft identities. It is increasingly unlikely that it will be possible or desirable to maintain the perceptions of difference encoded within these terms, as we enter an era characterized by greater cross-cultural exchange and the creation of new media that defy categorization as art or craft.

The greatest obstacle to the interpretation of crafts within a broader cultural context has been their exclusion from the mainstream art world. Ironically, while this external prejudice has fostered a sense of solidarity within the crafts community, it also has encouraged the perpetuation of marginalized status through an infrastructure of specialized schools, galleries, periodicals, critics, collectors, support groups, museums, and curators. Until craft institutions strike a balance between advocacy and the application of serious critical standards, and until mainstream institutions broaden their definitions of culture, this potent combination of pride and prejudice will continue to diminish the cultural landscape.

The contemporary crafts movement also has been hindered by the widespread perception that it is a uniquely American phenomenon of only a few decades' duration—a vision with enormous appeal in an era characterized by America's global cultural ascendancy and fascination with artistic innovation. This perception was facilitated by many American craft artists of the 1960s and 1970s, who unknowingly "reinvented" preexisting historical and contemporary techniques. While this condensed history has conferred greater short-term stature on this seemingly "new" movement and its artistic innovations, it has severed contemporary crafts from their historical foundations, thus diminishing their greater resonance, not only within the history of American art, but that of world culture.

Finally, the often adulatory focus on individual craft artists, along with an emphasis upon the seductive physical properties of specific media, has enabled personality and innovations to fill the void created by an absence of content in some craft objects.

Although the cult of personality and an exclusionary emphasis on the media of the moment also occur in the mainstream art world, the presence, absence, or quality of artistic content typically is tempered by a more extensive critical apparatus. This is not to argue that every (or any) object should make an overt or serious historical, political, or social statement, but rather to suggest that all objects resonate to a greater or lesser degree with historically derived meanings whose recovery has the potential to enrich both the object and its viewers. As the once distinct art and craft worlds continue to evolve and to converge, their proponents are likely to find common cause in objects that synthesize significant form with significant content—thus creating culturally resonant bearers of meaning.

Notes

This essay is dedicated to my wife, Kristin Triff Burgard, whose art-historical insights and editorial suggestions have greatly enhanced this publication.

1. Tina Oldknow, *Pilchuck: A Glass School* (Seattle: Pilchuck Glass School in association with University of Washington Press, 1996), 45–46.
2. Oldknow, *Pilchuck,* 43.
3. Oldknow, *Pilchuck,* 52.
4. Oldknow, *Pilchuck,* 20.
5. Oldknow, *Pilchuck,* 23, 106–9.
6. Oldknow, *Pilchuck,* 27.
7. Oldknow, *Pilchuck,* 51–52, 57, 66.
8. For Vallien's stay in the United States and Mexico, see Gunnar Lindquist, *Bertil Vallien,* trans. Angela Adegren (Stockholm: Gunnar Lindquist and Carlsson Bokförlag, 1990), 19–20.
9. Lindquist, *Bertil Vallien,* 33–35.
10. Lindquist, *Bertil Vallien,* 47.
11. *Dictionary of Art* (London: Grove, 1996), s.v. "Oseberg."
12. *Dictionary of Art,* s.v. "Viking Art: Decorative Arts."
13. Lindquist, *Bertil Vallien,* 127.
14. Lindquist, *Bertil Vallien,* 129.
15. Gunnar Lindquist, "Bertil Vallien: Glass Art Innovator, Metaphysical Explorer," *Neues Glas* 2 (1996): 23.
16. Bertil Vallien, "Sources of Inspiration: The Fading Newspaper Article, Area II," facsimile letter to William Traver Gallery, Seattle, Washington, 7 November 1998.
17. Vallien, "Sources of Inspiration."
18. Gary Blonston, *Artifacts/Glass* (New York: Abbeville Press, 1996), 10.
19. Narcissus Quagliata, afterword to Kate Elliot, ed., *William Morris Glass: Artifact and Art* (Seattle: University of Washington Press, 1989), 79, 82.
20. Patterson Sims, "Artifact and Art," in *William Morris Glass: Artifact and Art,* 10.
21. Patricia Failing, "William Morris: Glass Remains," *American Craft* 53 (February/ March 1993): 50.
22. Sims, "Artifact and Art," 9.
23. Liam Kelly, "The Work of Clifford Rainey," in *Clifford Rainey: Sculpture and Drawings, 1967–1987* (Belfast: Arts Council Gallery of Belfast, 1987), 4–6.
24. For an analysis of the cultural complexities associated with our perceptions of "primitivism" and "modernism," see James Clifford, *The Predicament of Culture: Twentieth-Century Ethnography, Literature, and Art* (Cambridge, Mass., and London: Harvard University Press, 1988).
25. Kelly, "Clifford Rainey," 5–6.

26. In a handwritten note dated 14 May 1990 from the Saxe Collection research files, Rainey described *Fetish*: "From a series 'Fetish' which uses the contemporary international icon as a symbol of metamorphosis between the past and the present. The sculpture is cast with re-cycled glass, mainly Coke bottles, to convey the conservation message."

27. Karen Tsujimoto, "Peter Voulkos: The Wood-Fired Work," in Rose Slivka and Karen Tsujimoto, *The Art of Peter Voulkos* (Tokyo: Kodansha International, in collaboration with The Oakland Museum, 1995), 111.

28. Tsujimoto, "Peter Voulkos," 114–17.

29. For additional examples of Voulkos's use of the triangle as a symbol for pyramids, see Slivka and Tsujimoto, *The Art of Peter Voulkos*, plates 54, 60, 75.

30. Tsujimoto, "Peter Voulkos," 108.

31. Tsujimoto, "Peter Voulkos," 121.

32. Tsujimoto, "Peter Voulkos," 121.

33. Tsujimoto, "Peter Voulkos," 119.

34. For a description of Voulkos's use of the *anagama,* and its characteristics, see Tsujimoto, "Peter Voulkos," 106–7, 109.

35. Rita Reif, "After 50 Years, Still Coaxing Secrets Out of Clay," *New York Times*, 14 April 1996.

36. Tsujimoto, "Peter Voulkos," 108.

37. Tsujimoto, "Peter Voulkos," 108.

38. Tsujimoto, "Peter Voulkos," 116–17.

39. Reif, "After 50 Years."

40. Tsujimoto, "Peter Voulkos," 100.

41. Embracing the Greek heritage of his immigrant parents, some of Voulkos's earliest works included disproportionately large reinterpretations of ancient Greek pottery, which he knew only through reproductions. See Thomas Albright, *Art in the San Francisco Bay Area, 1945–1980* (Berkeley: University of California Press, 1985), 135.

42. Laura Weir Hill and Scott Hill, "The Elevation of Ceramics: Robert Arneson and His Art," *Art of California* 6 (October 1993): 62.

43. Katharyn Regan, "Un-American Graffiti," *San Francisco* (April 1982): 46. For *No Deposit, No Return,* see Neal Benezra, *Robert Arneson: A Retrospective,* exh. cat. (Des Moines, Iowa: Des Moines Art Center, 1985), 18.

44. For *Self-Portrait of the Artist Losing His Marbles,* see *Robert Arneson: Self-Reflections,* exh. cat. (San Francisco: San Francisco Museum of Modern Art, 1997), 24–26.

45. Benezra, *Robert Arneson: A Retrospective*, 30, 32, 34.

46. Benezra, *Robert Arneson: A Retrospective*, 56.

47. Robert Arneson, written response to a questionnaire from the organizers of an exhibition of California artists, September 1982, cited in *Robert Arneson: Self-Reflections*, 10.

48. Robert Arneson, written statement in the artist's archives, September 1982, cited in *Robert Arneson: Self-Reflections*, 10.

49. Robert Arneson, "Alice Street and After," lecture at U.C. Davis, 1989, cited in *Robert Arneson: Self-Reflections*, 14.

50. Robert Arneson in conversation with Suzann Boettger, 28 December 1981, cited in Benezra, *Robert Arneson: A Retrospective*, 67.

51. For *California Artist,* see *Robert Arneson: Self-Reflections*, 40–43.

52. Ted Lindberg, "Stephen De Staebler," in *Stephen De Staebler: An Exhibition of Recent Bronzes Organized by The Emily Carr College of Art and Design, and The Art Museum Association of America,* exh. cat. (Vancouver, British Columbia: The Charles H. Scott Gallery, The Emily Carr College of Art and Design; San Francisco: The Art Museum Association of America, 1983), 6.

53. Dore Ashton, "Objects Worked by the Imagination for Their Innerness: The Sculpture of Stephen De Staebler," *Arts Magazine* 59 (November 1984): 141.

54. Ashton, "Objects Worked by the Imagination," 142.

55. Lindberg, "Stephen De Staebler," 24.

56. Ramsay Bell Breslin, "The Figure as a Fragment: The Sculpture of Stephen De Staebler," in *Stephen De Staebler: Recent Work, August 30–October 1, 1994* (San Francisco: Campbell-Thiebaud Gallery, 1994).

57. Ashton, "Objects Worked by the Imagination," 144.

58. Arthur C. Danto, "Illusion and Comedy: The Art of John Cederquist," in Arthur C. Danto and Nancy Princenthal, *The Art of John Cederquist: Reality of Illusion* (Oakland: Oakland Museum of California, 1997), 10.

59. Sharon K. Emanuelli, "John Cederquist: Deceptions," *American Craft* 43 (October/November 1983): 24.

60. Kenneth R. Trapp, introduction, in Danto and Princenthal, *Art of John Cederquist,* 9.

61. Kate Rothrock, biography, in Danto and Princenthal, *Art of John Cederquist,* 129.

62. Danto, "Illusion and Comedy," 16–17.

63. Rothrock, biography, 129.

64. In 1989, Cederquist made a deconstructed version of a colonial Newport, Rhode Island, high chest by John Townsend (1732–1809), in the permanent collection of the Museum of Fine Arts, Boston. See Cederquist's *Le Fleuron Manquant* (The Missing Finial) in *New American Furniture: The Second Generation of Studio Furnituremakers* (Boston: Museum of Fine Arts; Edward S. Cooke, Jr., 1989), 40–43.

65. Rothrock, biography, 128.

66. Trapp, introduction, 8, 23.

67. *Hokusai and Hiroshige: Great Japanese Prints from the James A. Michener Collection,* exh. cat. (San Francisco: The Asian Art Museum of San Francisco, in association with the Honolulu Academy of Arts and University of Washington Press, 1998), 37.

68. For Hokusai's print series *A Tour of Japanese Waterfalls,* see *Hokusai and Hiroshige,* 101–10.

69. For Hokusai's *Waterwheel at Onden,* see *Hokusai and Hiroshige,* 80.

70. Conversation with the artist, 14 January 1999.

71. *Hokusai and Hiroshige,* 32.

72. Helaine Posner, *Kiki Smith* (Boston: Bulfinch Press/Little, Brown and Company, 1998), 11.

73. Helaine Posner, "Approaching Grace," in Posner, *Kiki Smith,* 11.

74. Posner, "Approaching Grace," 25.

75. David Frankel, "In Her Own Words," in Posner, *Kiki Smith,* 37.

76. Posner, "Approaching Grace," 16.

77. Posner, "Approaching Grace," 19.

78. Kirk Varnedoe, *Jasper Johns: A Retrospective,* exh. cat. (New York: The Museum of Modern Art, 1996), plates 91–94, 212–13.

79. Posner, "Approaching Grace," 8, 9, 16.

80. See *Lienzo of Ihuitlan,* illustrated in Diana Fane, ed., *Converging Cultures: Art & Identity in Spanish America* (New York: The Brooklyn Museum, in association with Harry N. Abrams, Inc., 1996), 77.

81. See Posner, *Kiki Smith,* 75.

82. Posner, "Approaching Grace," 18.

83. Janet Kutner, "Free Association with the Human Body," *Dallas Morning News,* 19 January 1989.

84. Posner, "Approaching Grace," 13.

CATALOGUE OF THE COLLECTION

NARCISSUS QUAGLIATA

Left: *George Saxe: Portrait in Glass*, 1990
   Leaded blown-glass panel, 72¾ × 42⅛ in.
Right: *Dorothy Saxe: Portrait in Glass*, 1990
   Leaded blown-glass panel, 67½ × 34 in.

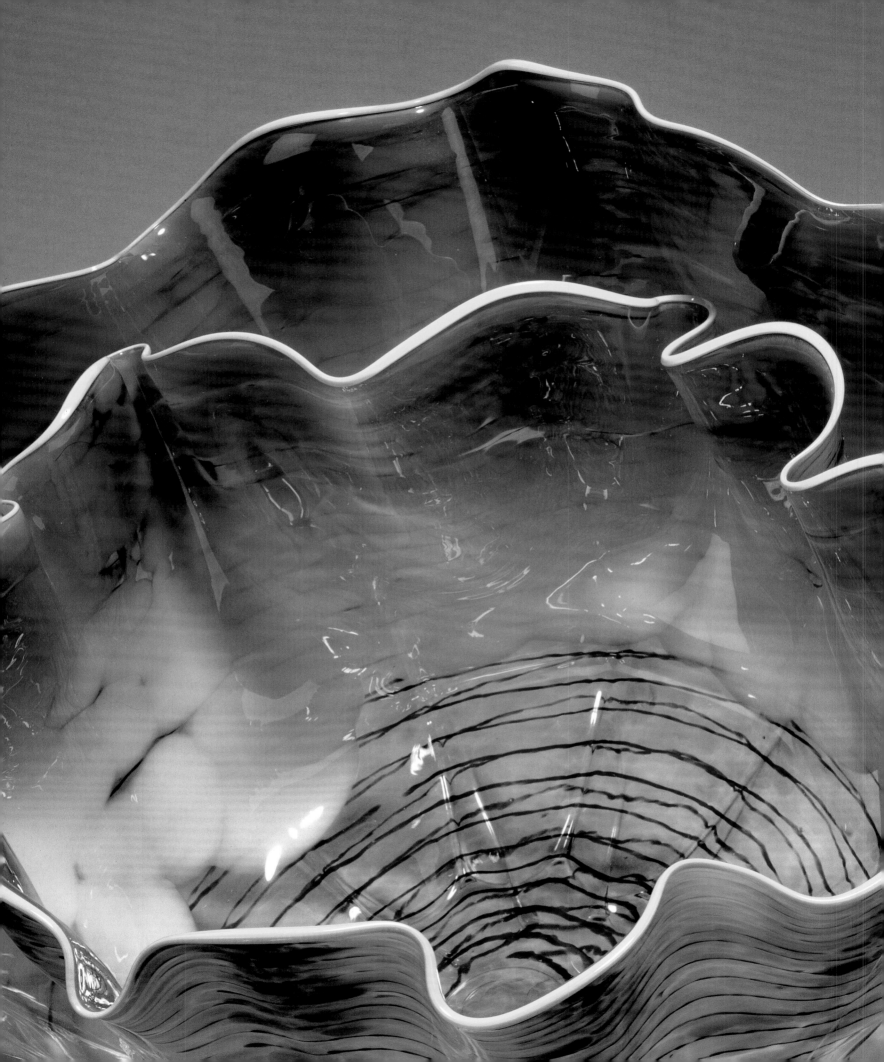

GLASS

Dominick Labino

Emergence in Polychrome, 1981

Blown glass, 7¹⁄₁₆ × 3¾ × 2⅛ in.

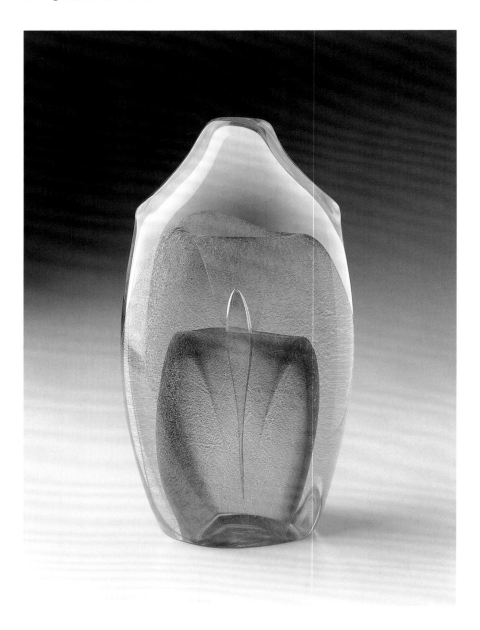

HARVEY K. LITTLETON
300° Rotated Ellipsoid, 1980
Blown glass
Left: 14¾ × 6 × 6 in.
Right: 3⅝ × 6⅝ × 3⅝ in.

opposite:

LINO TAGLIAPIETRA
Dinosaur, 1997
Blown glass, 36 × 13 × 5 in.

MARVIN LIPOFSKY
Seattle Series #3, 1990–94
Blown glass, 14¾ × 16 × 14½ in.

THOMAS PATTI
Split Ascending Red, 1990
Float glass, 5⁵⁄₁₆ × 4⅞ × 3 in.

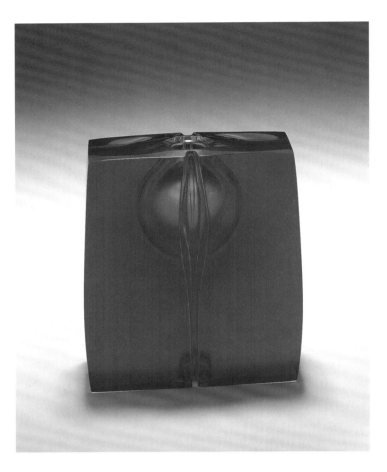

THOMAS PATTI
Planular Gray Solar Riser, 1981
Plate glass, 6 × 5⅜ × 2⅜ in.

Thomas Patti

Spectral Starphire with Amber, Blue, Green, Red, and Black, 1996

Float glass, 4¹⁄₁₆ × 6¼ × 4⁷⁄₁₆ in.

ZOLTÁN BOHUS

Architectonic Element, 1985

Anodized and laminated plate glass, 10½ × 17⅞ × 9⅞ in.

De Wain Valentine

Open Diamond Rotated Hyperbolic Parabola, 1985

Plate glass, 18 × 34¼ × 14¾ in.

FRANTISEK VÍZNER

Smoked Bowl, 1992

Cast glass, 3¼ × 11¼ in. diameter

FRANTISEK VÍZNER

Gold Bowl, 1993

Cast glass, 4⅛ × 11½ in. diameter

MARK PEISER

Lover's Leap, 1980

Blown glass, 12½ × 5¾ in.

MARK PEISER

Mountain Skyscape, 1993

Blown glass, 8 × 18 × 3 in.

ANN WÄRFF WOLFF
Viklauska, 1987
Glass, steel, and granite, 30⅛ × 9⅛ × 11 in.

opposite:
ANN WÄRFF WOLFF
Game Rondell, 1985
Glass and granite, 27¼ × 20¼ × 18¾ in.

JON KUHN
Portal of Andromeda, 1990
Cast and laminated glass, 15⅝ × 11¾ × 12½ in.

opposite:
LARRY BELL
Untitled, 1986
Glass and rhodium-plated brass, 14⅛ in. square cube,
on a Plexiglas base, 36 × 14 × 14 in.

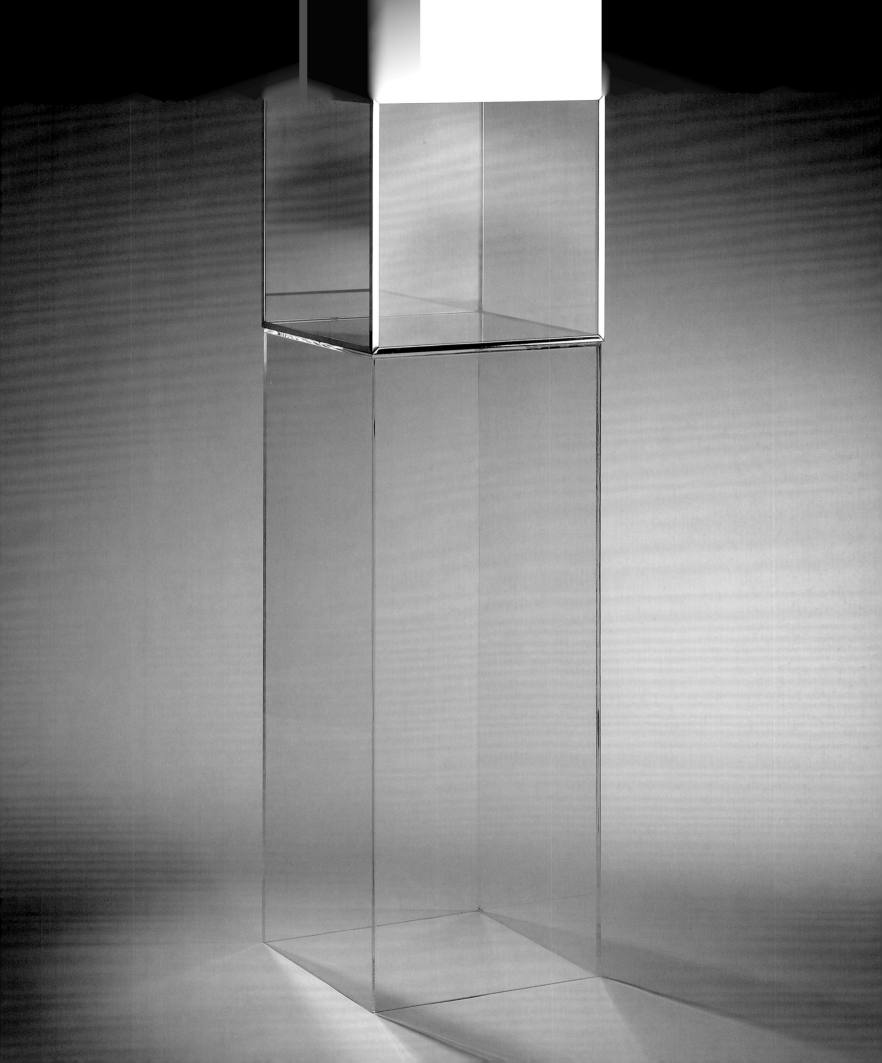

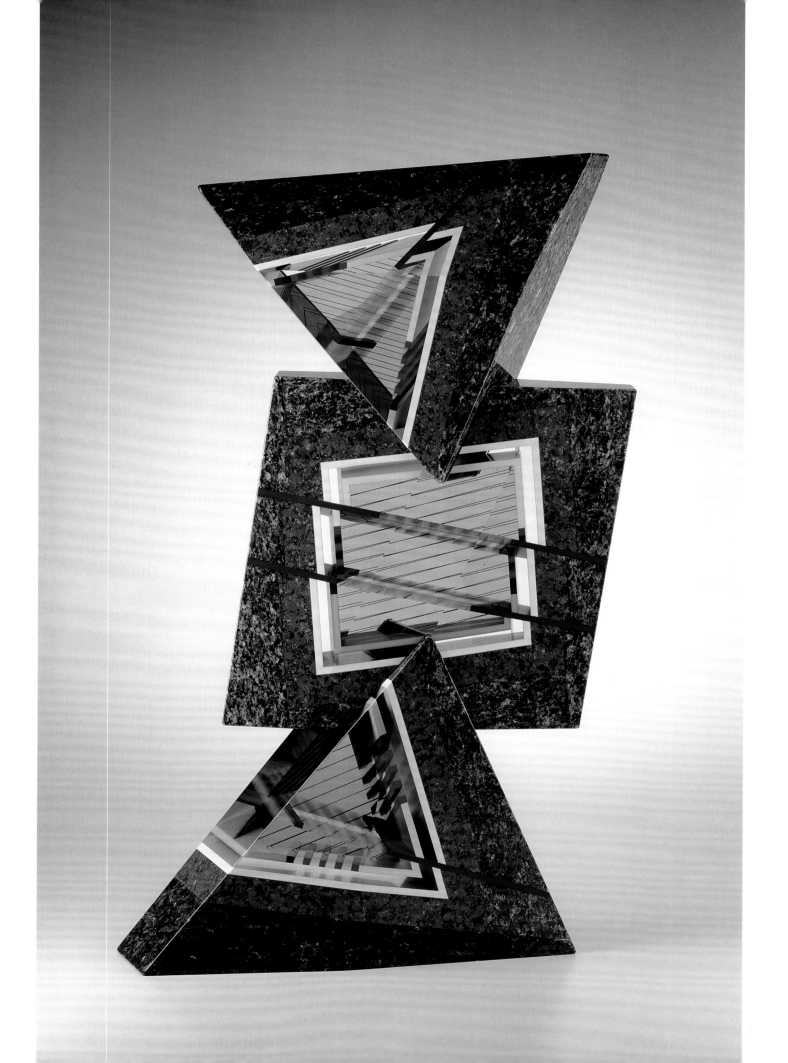

opposite:

WILLIAM CARLSON

Pragnanz, 1991

Cast glass, Vitriolite, granite, and wire, 33½ × 19⅝ × 9½ in.

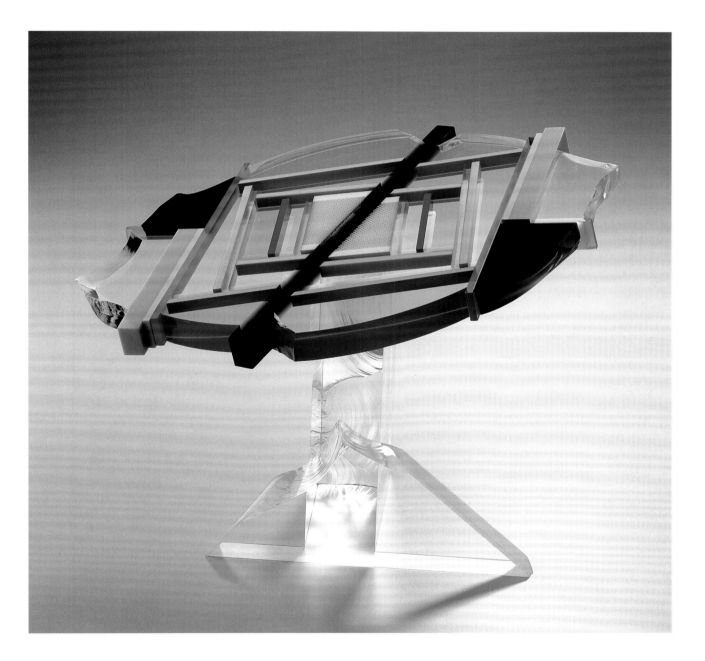

DAVID R. HUCHTHAUSEN

Uranium Chrysalis, 1990

Sheet glass and Vitriolite, 12¼ × 18 × 13¼ in.

Michael Glancy

Cerise Star X, 1988

Blown glass, plate glass, and copper

Bowl: 3¾ × 10½ in. diameter

Base: ¾ × 15¹⁄₁₆ × 15¹⁄₁₆ in., on a Plexiglas base,

    ¾ × 10¼ × 9½ in.

opposite:

Brian Hirst

Object and Image Series—Votive, 1994

Blown glass, gold, and enamel

Vessel: 11⅝ × 14¼ × 14¼ in.

Panel: 41⅝ × 26⅛ × 1¼ in.

KYOHEI FUJITA
Red and White Plum Blossoms, 1998
Mold-blown glass, silver, and gold and platinum
leaf, 6½ × 6½ in. diameter

Mary Ann (Toots) Zynsky

Untitled, 1991
Fused glass, 5⅞ × 13½ × 7¾ in.

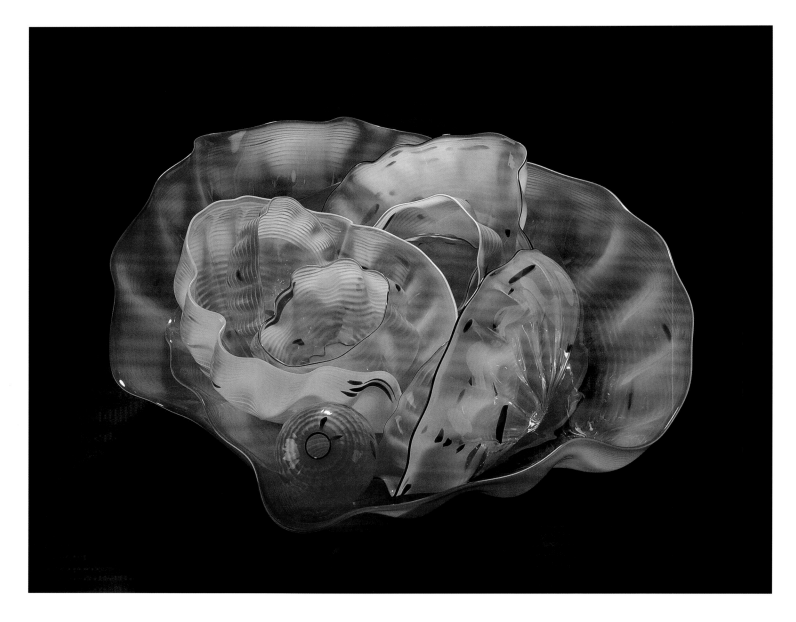

DALE CHIHULY
Pink Seaform Set, 1982/90
Blown glass, 13½ × 32 × 25 in.

DALE CHIHULY

Black Set, 1980

Blown glass, 6¾ × 16 × 15 in.

opposite:

DALE CHIHULY
Bright Turquoise Soft Cylinder with Yellow Lip Wrap, 1992
Blown glass, 21 × 15⅞ × 17 in.

DALE CHIHULY
Prussian Green Macchia Pair with Cadmium Yellow Lip Wrap, 1986
Blown glass, 14¹¹⁄₁₆ × 27 × 21 in.

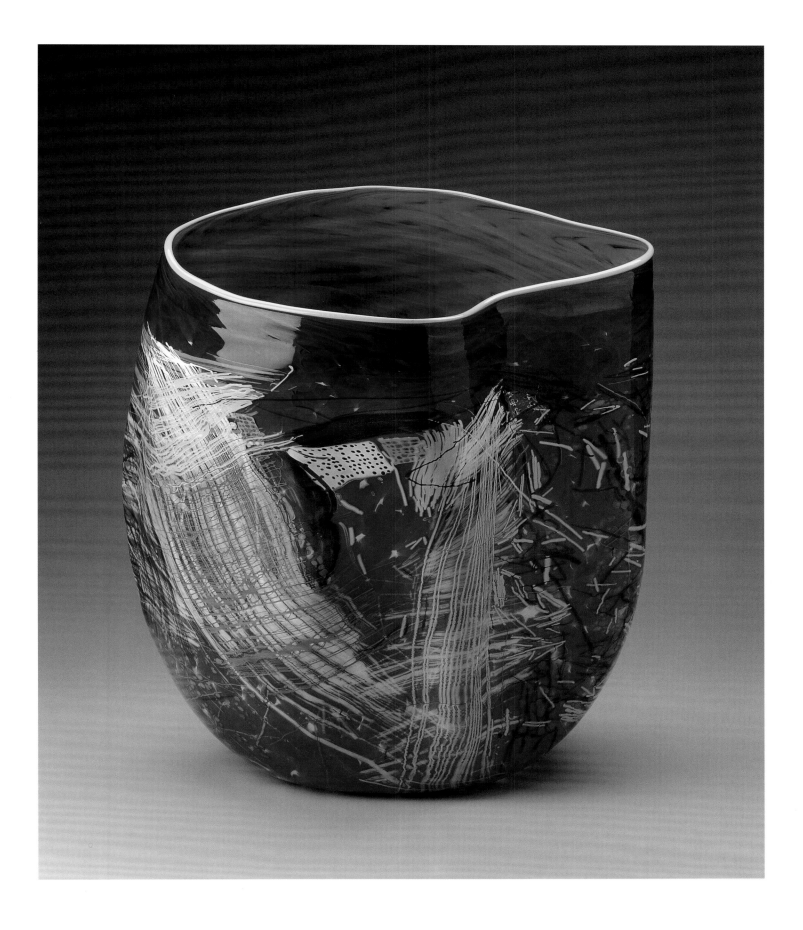

Dale Chihuly

Ultramarine Stemmed Form with Orange (Persian Series), 1988
Blown glass, 22³/₁₆ × 43¼ × 23¼ in.

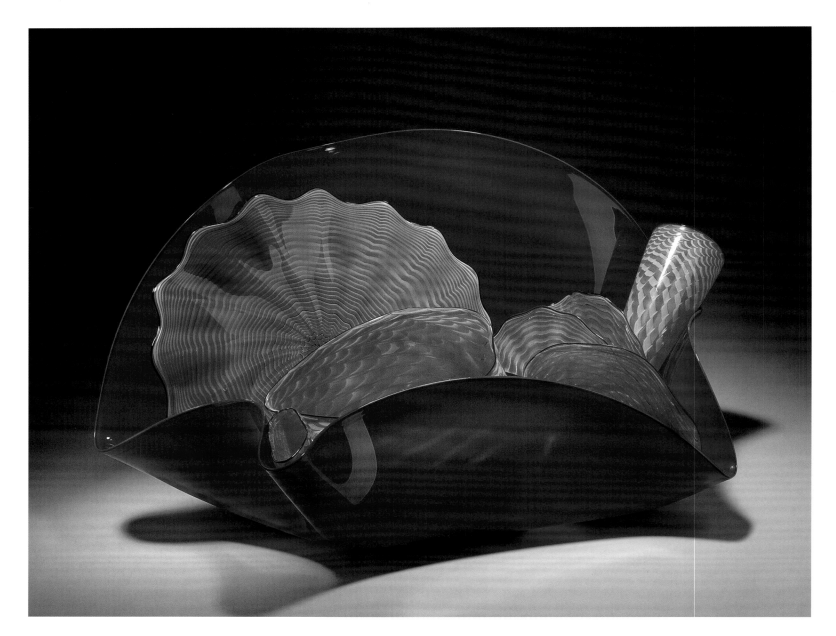

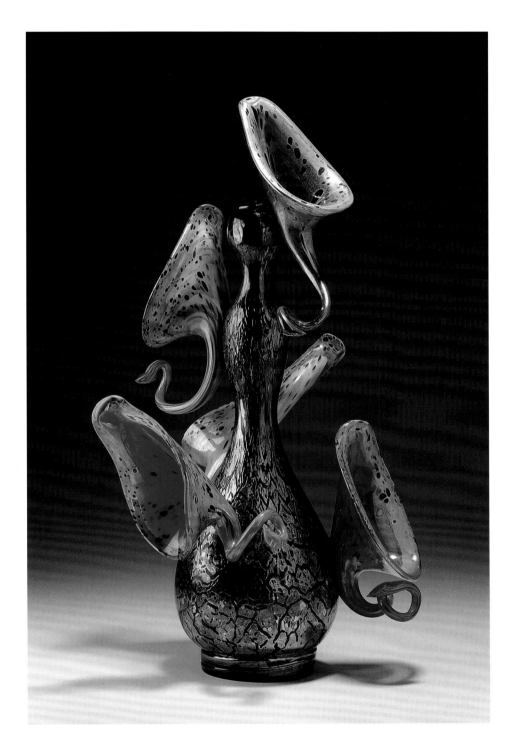

DALE CHIHULY

Gold over Cobalt Venetian, 1989

Blown glass, 25¾ × 13 × 11½ in.

DALE CHIHULY
Geranium Red Venetian with Terre Verte
Leaves and Oxide of Chromium Rings, 1989
Blown glass, 20½ × 14¾ × 12 in.

opposite:
DALE CHIHULY
Green Leaf Venetian, 1990
Blown glass, 23¼ × 14½ × 17¼ in.

opposite:

DALE CHIHULY

Gilded Black Ikebana Vase with Three Stems, 1992

Blown glass, 51¾ × 33½ × 18¾ in.

DALE CHIHULY

Left: *Mottled Black Float,* 1992

    Blown glass, 16 × 17 × 17 in.

Right: *Gilded Silver Black Float,* 1992

    Blown glass, 22 × 19½ × 19½ in.

KLAUS MOJE

Lifesaver (Bowl #2), 1979

Fused glass, 2⅛ × 8¹¹⁄₁₆ in. diameter

KLAUS MOJE

Untitled Bowl #3, 1984

Fused glass, 2⅛ × 13 × 12¹³⁄₁₆ in.

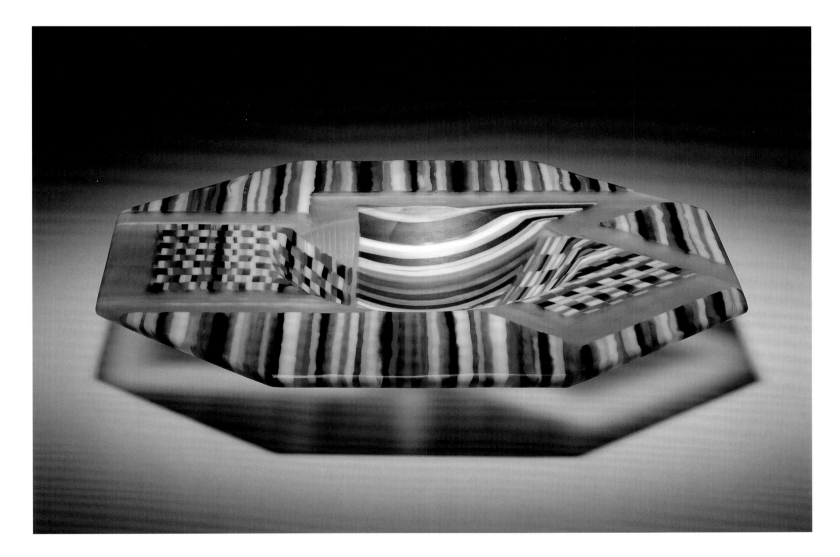

KLAUS MOJE

Untitled (#37), 1990

Fused glass, 3 × 20⅞ in. diameter

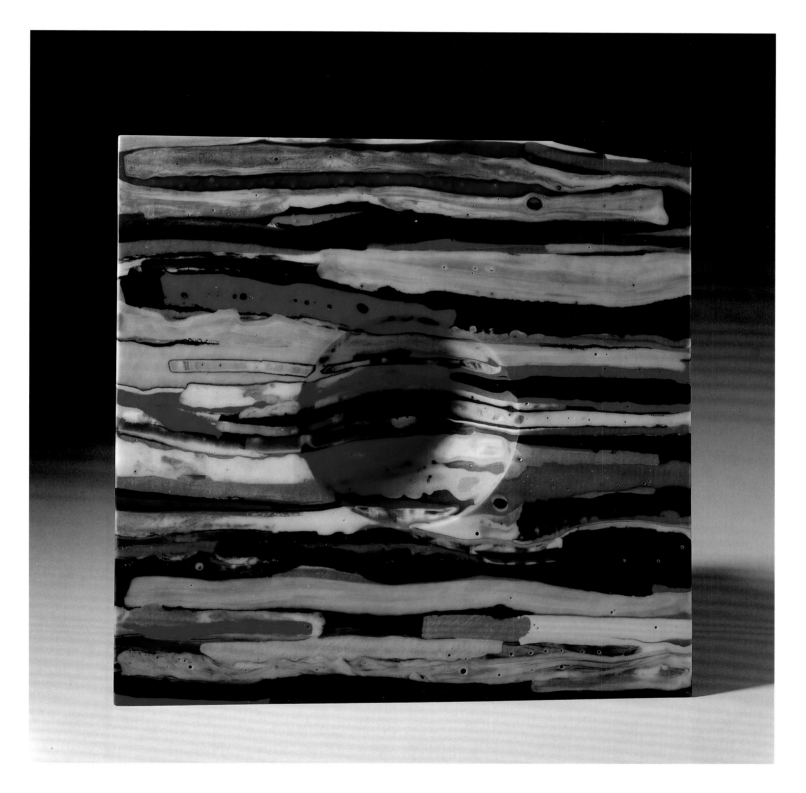

Klaus Moje
Untitled (#7), 1991
Fused glass, 2¼ × 17¼ × 17⅟₁₆ in.

JOEL PHILIP MYERS
CFOURBLUEBRG, 1989
Blown glass, 14 × 15 × 3 in.

JOEL PHILIP MYERS

CFNEOLONGJPM, 1989

Blown glass, 8⅝ × 32 × 3 in.

THERMAN STATOM
Seattle Ladder, 1992
Plate glass, blown glass, glass
fragments, paint, and silicone,
84 × 16⅞ × 4½ in.

GINNY RUFFNER

San Francisco Commission, 1991

Glass and paint, 13 × 20¾ × 10½ in.

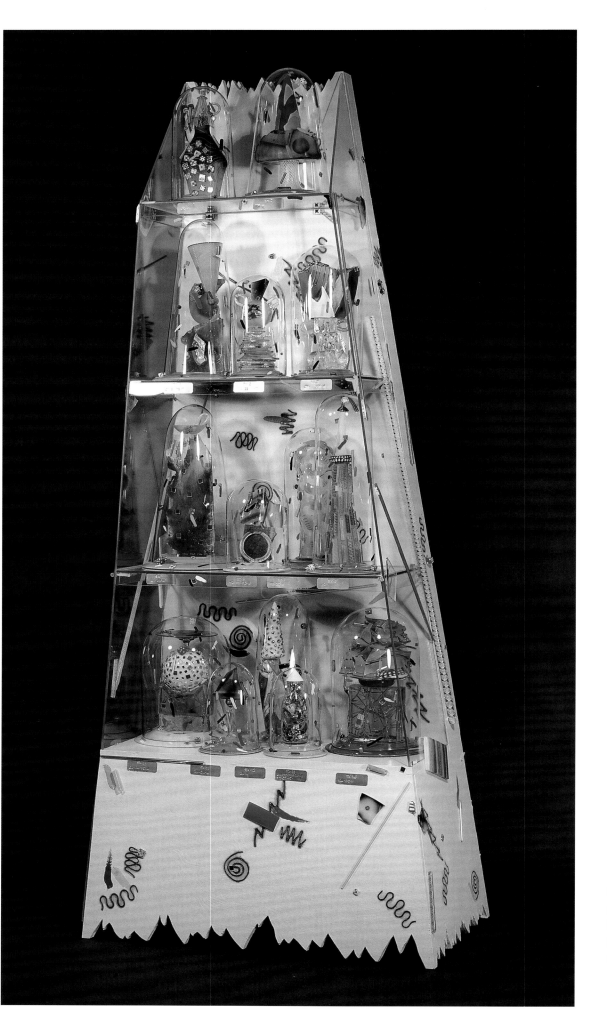

RICHARD MARQUIS

7.1, 1991

Blown glass jars, glass fragments,
Fiestaware plates, plywood, and
enamel paint, 85½ × 34 × 20 in.

RICHARD MARQUIS

Glass Cup, 1979

Glass, 2¾ × 7½ × 4 in.

WILLIAM MORRIS

Jar with Raven and Frogs, 1999

Blown glass, 19 × 16 × 13 in.

WILLIAM MORRIS

Artifact Still Life, 1989–90

Blown glass, scavo, gold leaf, and copper, 15¼ × 44 × 22 in.

WILLIAM MORRIS

Artifact: Tooth, 1996

Blown glass, 13¾ × 23 × 8½ in.

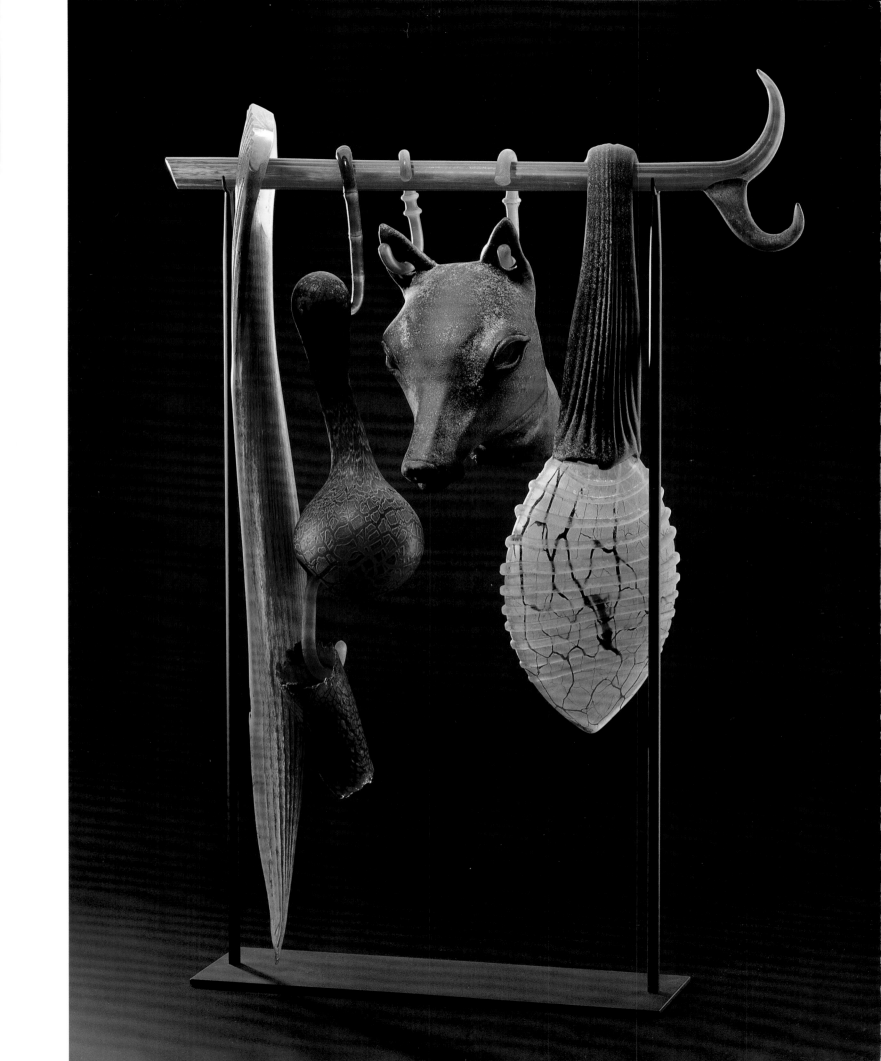

WILLIAM MORRIS

Petroglyph Urn with Horn, 1992

Blown glass, 24⅜ × 33 × 6½ in., on a steel stand, 20¼ × 23 × 5 in.

(verso)

WILLIAM MORRIS

Petroglyph Urn with Horn, 1992

Blown glass, 24⅜ × 33 × 6½ in., on a steel stand, 20¼ × 23 × 5 in.

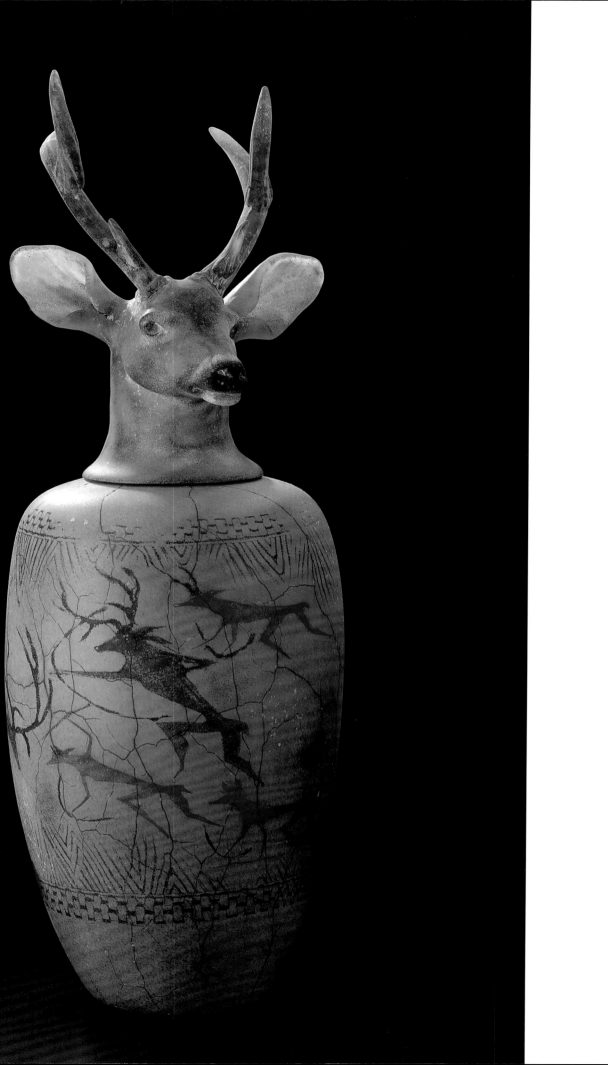

WILLIAM MORRIS

Rhyton: Mastodon, 1996

Blown glass, 12½ × 16 × 5¾ in.

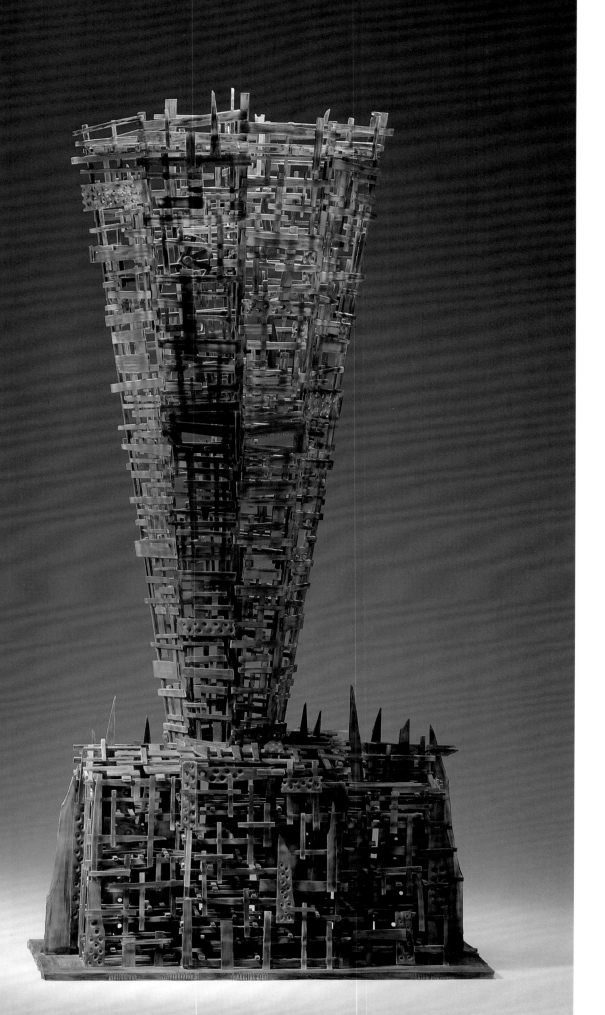

JAY MUSLER
Excoriated for His Mistake, 1985
Plate glass and pigment, 41½ ×
20½ × 9½ in.

KARLA TRINKLEY

Spiral Bowl, 1991

Pâte de verre, 15 × 18½ in. diameter

KARLA TRINKLEY

Cake, 1984

Pâte de verre, 8 × 9½ in. diameter

BRETISLAV NOVAK, JR.

Propeller, 1983

Cast glass, 10⅛ × 18⅜ × 12½ in.

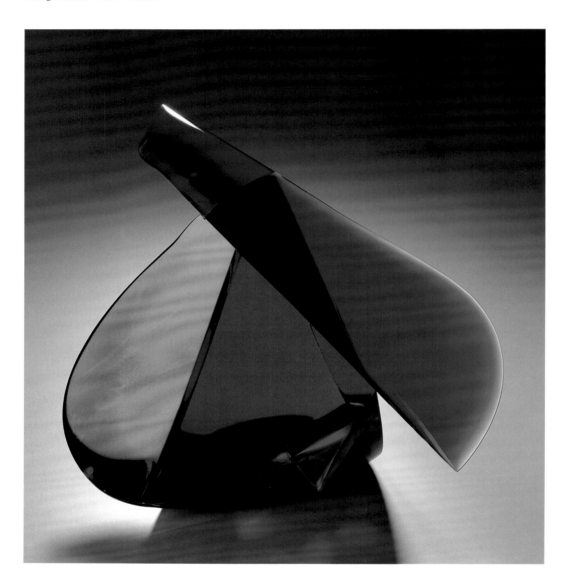

BETTY WOODMAN

Triptych A, 1993–96

Blown glass

Left: 22 × 19¾ × 6 in.

Center: 16 × 21½ × 6 in.

Right: 23¼ × 17 × 6¾ in.

STANISLAV LIBENSKÝ AND JAROSLAVA BRYCHTOVÁ

Open Window, 1992

Cast glass, 34 × 33 × 10 in.

**Stanislav Libenský and
Jaroslava Brychtová**
Flowering Throne, 1991
Cast glass, 42 × 15³⁄₁₆ × 8 in.

opposite:
Howard Ben Tré
First Figure, 1986
Sand-cast glass, brass, copper
leaf, and patina, 70¾ × 28½ × 9 in.

HOWARD BEN TRÉ

Cast Form Type V, #3479, 1979

Sand-cast glass, copper inlay, and patina,

6½ × 5⅛ × 3⁷⁄₁₆ in.

HOWARD BEN TRÉ

Cast Form Type IV, 1979

Sand-cast glass, copper inlay, and patina, 5⅝ × 7½ × 4⅞ in.

opposite:

HANK MURTA ADAMS

Siggy, 1986

Sand-cast glass, blown glass, enamel, and copper wire,
20 × 11½ × 14 in., on a wooden base, 2 × 8¾ × 8⅝ in.

LYNDA BENGLIS

Zita, 1984

Sand-cast glass, copper, and pigment, 8¼ × 13½ × 13⅛ in.

NICOLAS AFRICANO

Woman Eating Fruit, 1997
Cast glass, 15 × 8³⁄₁₆ × 8³⁄₈ in.

JANUSZ WALENTYNOWICZ

I Forgive You, 1991
Cast glass, 19½ × 26⅝ × 4 in.

DANA ZÁMEČNÍKOVÁ

Memory, 1991

Sheet glass, wire, lead, and paint, 20¾ × 19¼ × 9 in.

opposite:

MARI MÉSZÁROS

Bad Girls Go to Heaven, 1997

Glass, stone, and steel, 40½ × 18 × 13 in.

opposite:

CHRISTOPHER WILMARTH
My Old Books Closed, 1980–81
Blown glass and bronze, 24 × 15¹⁵⁄₁₆ × 4¾ in.

DANIEL CLAYMAN
Contrivance, 1992
Cast glass and copper, 26¼ × 9¼ × 1½ in.

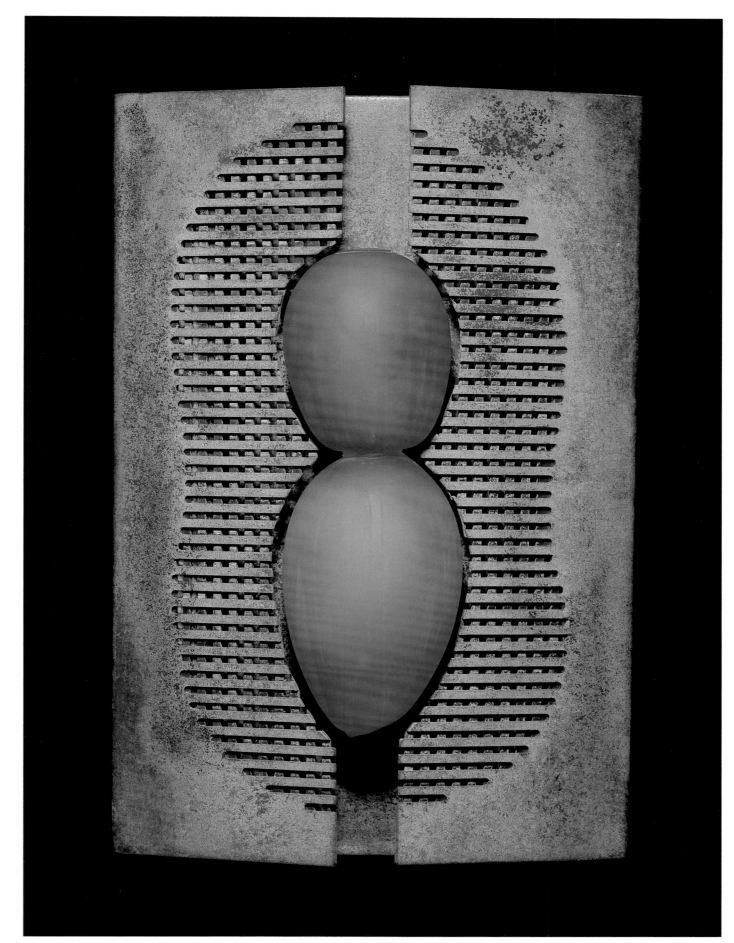

FLORA C. MACE AND JOEY KIRKPATRICK

Watercatcher, 1995

Blown glass, alder, and steel, 58½ × 28½ × 15½ in.

FLORA C. MACE AND JOEY KIRKPATRICK

Still Life, 1997

Blown glass and alder, 31 × 59 in. diameter

Dan Dailey

Baboon (no. 14), 1994

Blown glass, 15¼ × 11½ × 12 in.

opposite:

Dan Dailey

Minotaurs, 1997

Blown glass, Vitriolite, bronze, and gold-plated

bronze, 14¼ × 14 × 9¾ in.

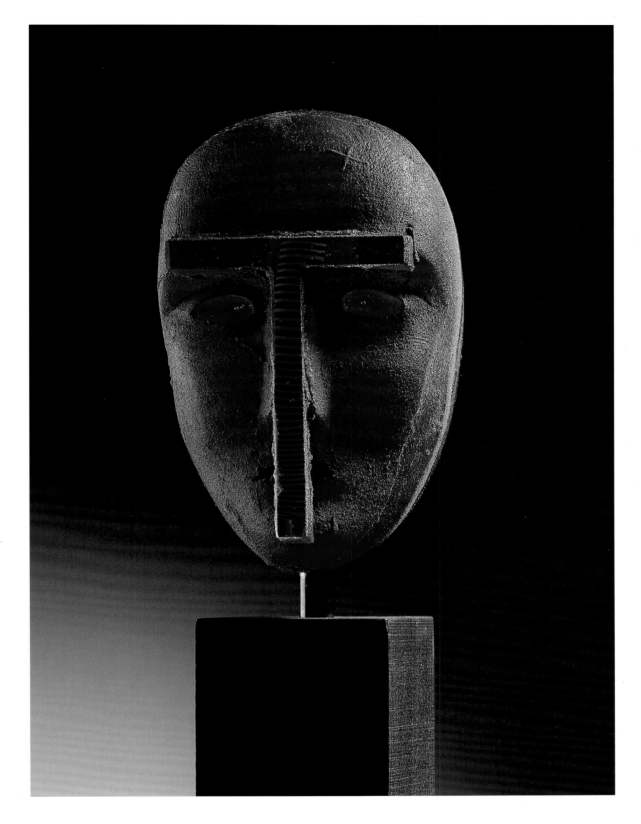

119

opposite:

BERTIL VALLIEN

Map IV, 1998

Sand-cast glass, steel, and copper, 26 × 30 × 10 in.,

on a steel base, 15⅜ × 27⅜ × 9¹³⁄₁₆ in.

BERTIL VALLIEN

Map IV, 1998

Sand-cast glass, steel, and copper, 26 × 30 × 10 in.,

on a steel base, 15⅜ × 27⅜ × 9¹³⁄₁₆ in.

(verso)

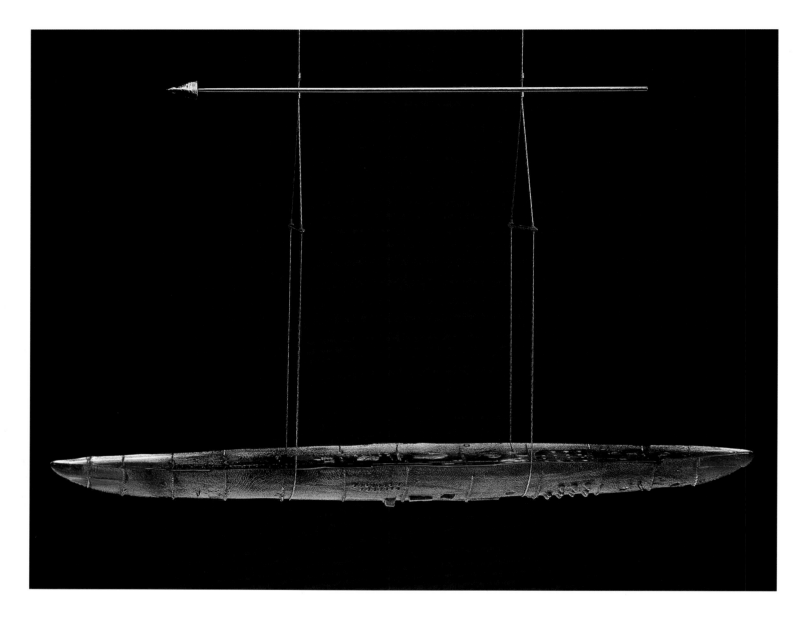

BERTIL VALLIEN

Bellagio, 1993

Sand-cast glass, steel, and wire, 33 (vessel and arrow) × 53 × 8 in.

BERTIL VALLIEN

Bellagio, 1993

Sand-cast glass, steel, and wire, 33 (vessel and arrow) × 53 × 8 in.

(detail)

Bertil Vallien
Atlantis, 1985
Sand-cast glass, 4 × 21⅛ × 10½ in.

opposite:

Clifford Rainey
Freedom of Conscience, 1989
Cast glass, wooden rulers, wood,
chain, and nails, 23½ × 13⅛ × 13¼ in.

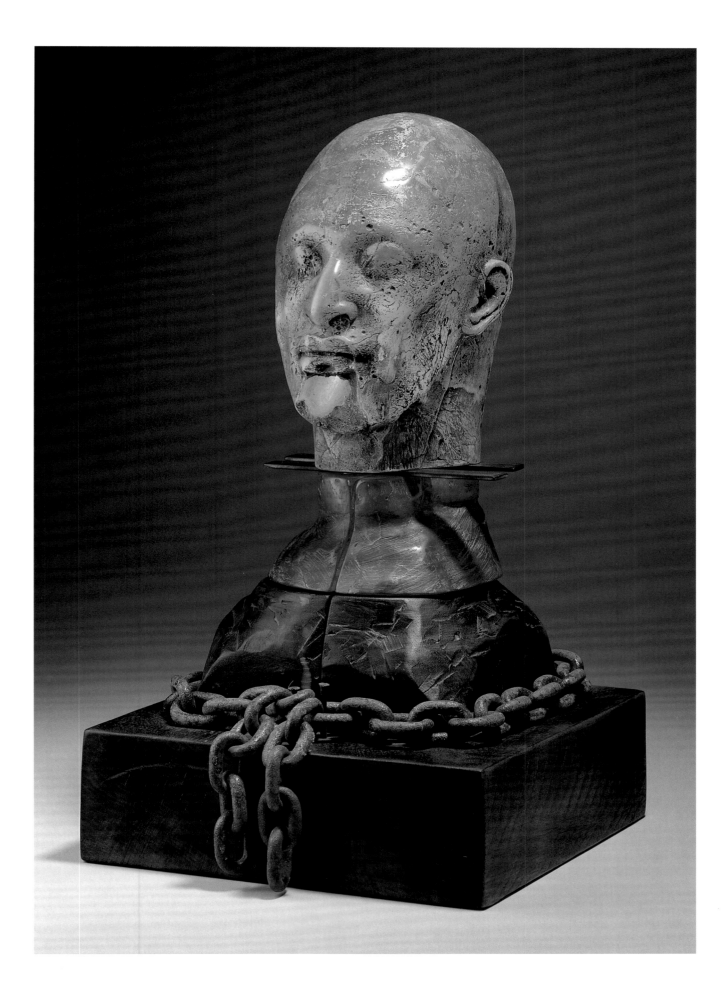

CLIFFORD RAINEY
Through the Looking Glass, 1992
Blown glass and iron wire
Cup: 9 × 13¼ × 10½ in.
Plate: 3 × 15¼ × 14½ in.

CLIFFORD RAINEY

Fetish, 1990

Cast recycled glass, iron nails, glass beads, steel
wire, wood, and oil paint, 39½ × 10 × 9½ in.

opposite:

ITALO SCANGA AND DALE CHIHULY

Rover's Garden Grows, 1991

Blown glass, steel, and acrylic paint, 68⅜ × 66⅝ × 21¾ in.

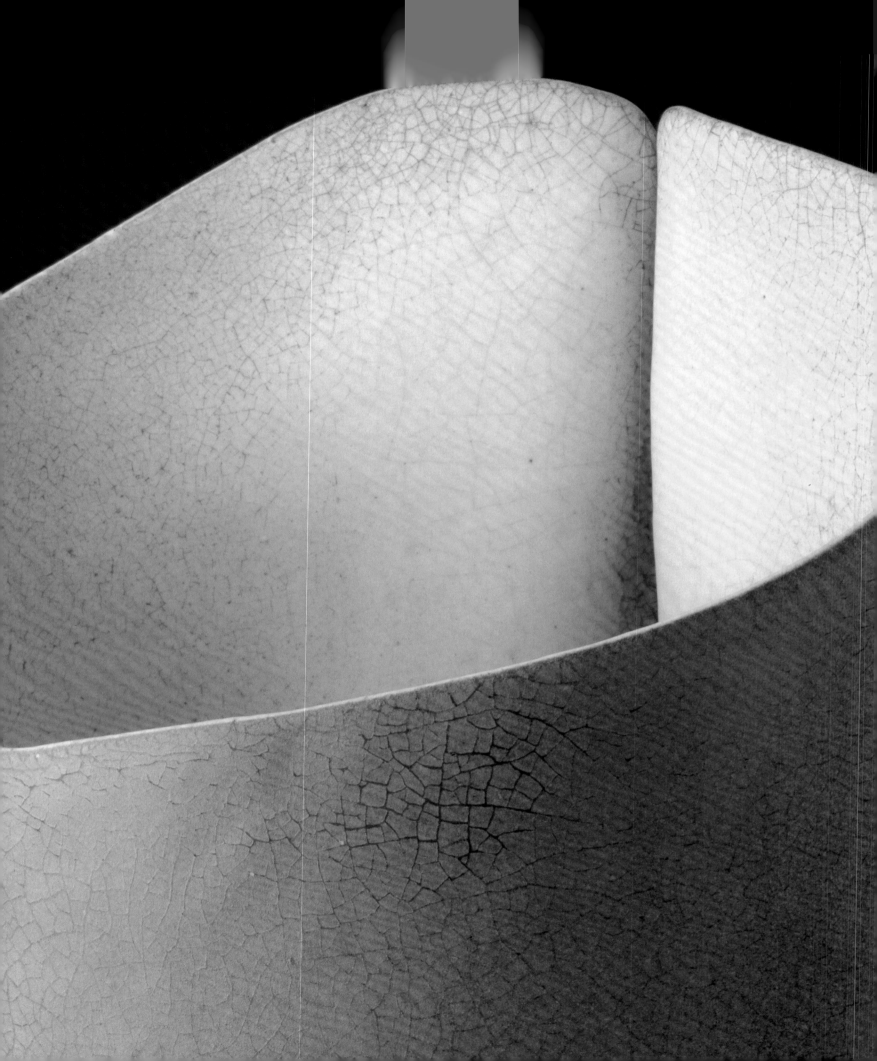

CERAMIC

PAUL SOLDNER

#976, 1997

Raku-fired earthenware, 27½ × 30¼ × 10½ in.,

on a steel base, 1¼ × 11½ in. diameter

PAUL SOLDNER

Untitled, 1985

Raku-fired earthenware, 18½ × 11½ × 6¾ in.

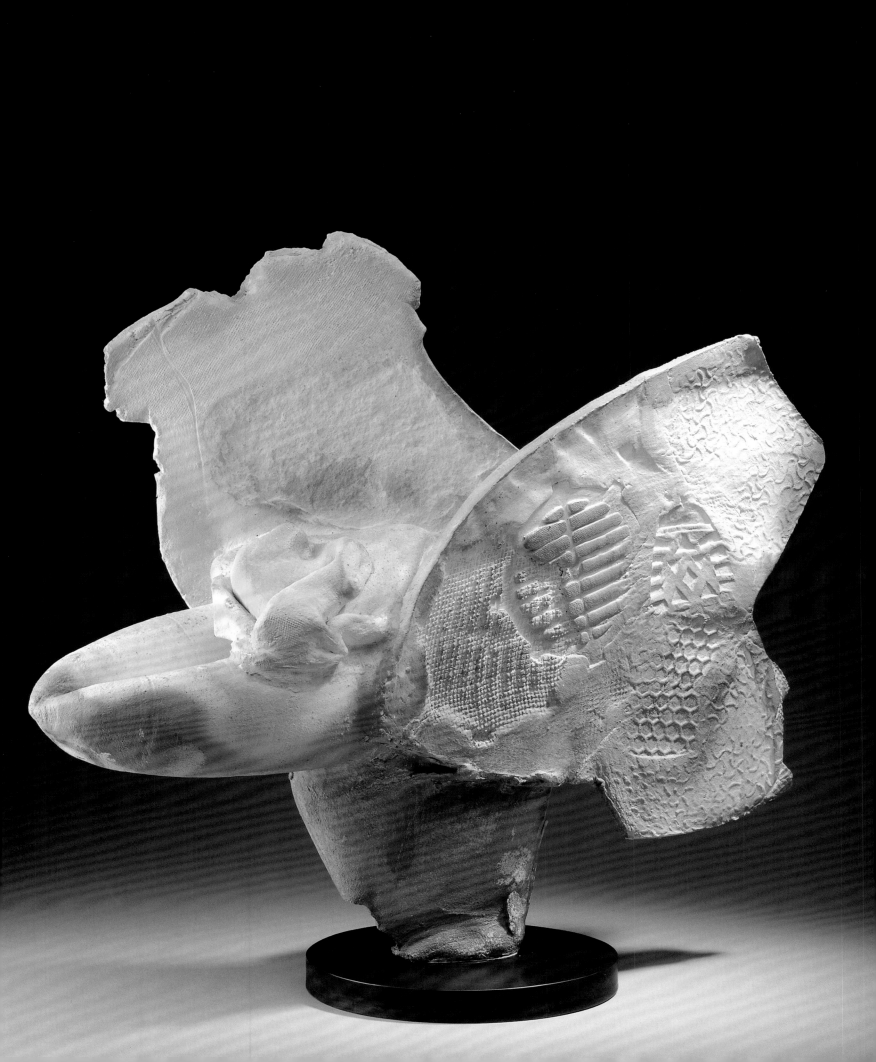

opposite:

DANIEL RHODES
Guardian Figure—Regla, 1988
Glazed stoneware, 48¾ × 19 × 12 in.

DANIEL RHODES
Abique #245, 1988
Stoneware, 16½ × 17 × 23 in.

opposite:

PETER VOULKOS
Yogi, 1997
Stoneware, 46 × 32 × 25 in.

PETER VOULKOS
Untitled (Stack), 1980
Stoneware, 46 × 15 in. diameter

Peter Voulkos
Untitled (Plate), 1981
Stoneware, 4 × 20¼ in. diameter

ROBERT TURNER
Shore, 1989
Glazed stoneware and slip, 11 × 8 × 8 in.

Robert Turner

Form IV, 1989

Glazed stoneware and slip, 10½ × 9½ in. diameter

ROBERT SPERRY
Untitled (#794), 1987
Glazed stoneware and slip, 4 × 27 in. diameter

CHRISTINA BERTONI
By This Immovability All Things Are Moved, 1987
Earthenware and acrylic paint, 7 × 17⅜ × 9⅞ in.

JUN KANEKO
Untitled, ca. 1983
Glazed stoneware, 3⅛ × 24¾ × 20¾ in.

JERRY ROTHMAN

Classic Baroque Tureen, 1978
Glazed porcelain, 16⅝ × 17 × 9 in.

ADRIAN SAXE

Left: *Untitled Ewer 91-206,* 1991
    Glazed porcelain and fishing lure, 13⅜ × 9 × 3¾ in.

Right: *Untitled (Teapot 92-208),* 1991
    Glazed porcelain and glass pendant, 11½ × 8 in.

opposite:

ADRIAN SAXE

Antelope Jar, 1982
Glazed porcelain and stoneware, 25¾ × 11½ × 6⅛ in.

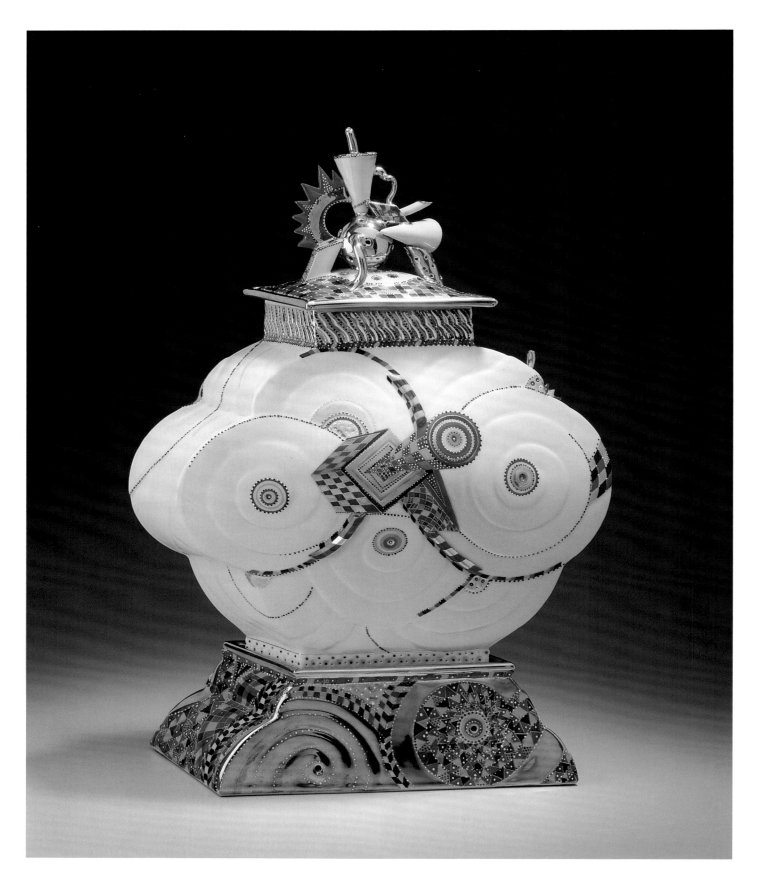

RALPH BACERRA

Cloud Vessel, 1996
Glazed porcelain, 23⅝ × 16½ × 6½ in.

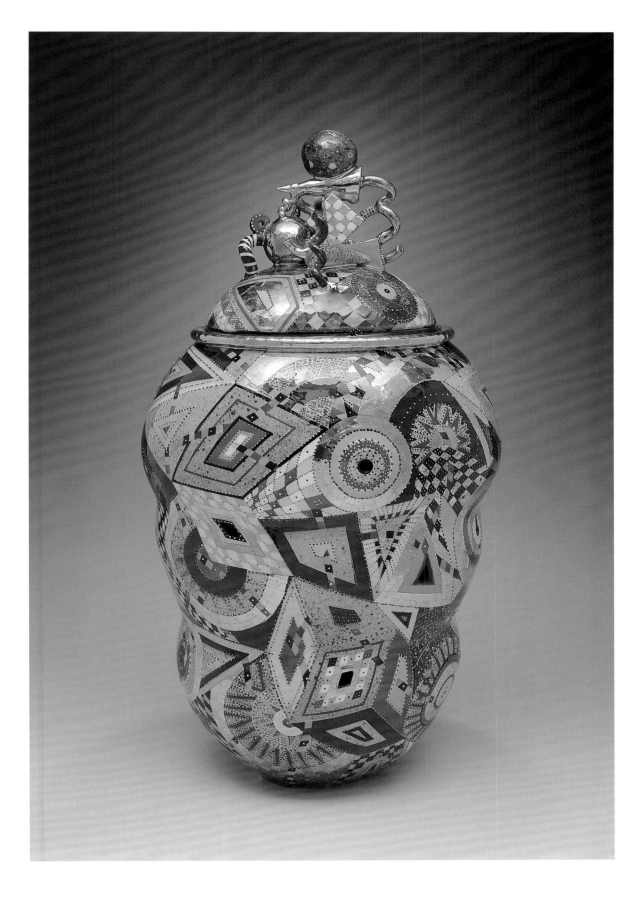

RALPH BACERRA

Large Lidded Jar, 1998

Glazed earthenware, 25½ × 13½ in.

diameter

opposite:

BETTY WOODMAN

Pillow Pitcher, 1990

Glazed earthenware, 22⅞ × 23¼ × 14½ in.

BETTY WOODMAN

Hydra Cactus (Triptych), 1990

Glazed earthenware

Left: 27½ × 14¾ × 7¾ in.

Center: 27¼ × 25¼ × 8 in.

Right: 27 × 23 × 8 in.

opposite:

RICHARD DeVore

#782, 1995

Glazed stoneware, 16 × 11 × 9¾ in.

BENNETT BEAN

Bean Bowl #154, 1990

Glazed earthenware, terra sigillata, gold leaf,

and acrylic paint, 8⅝ × 15¾ × 14⅞ in.

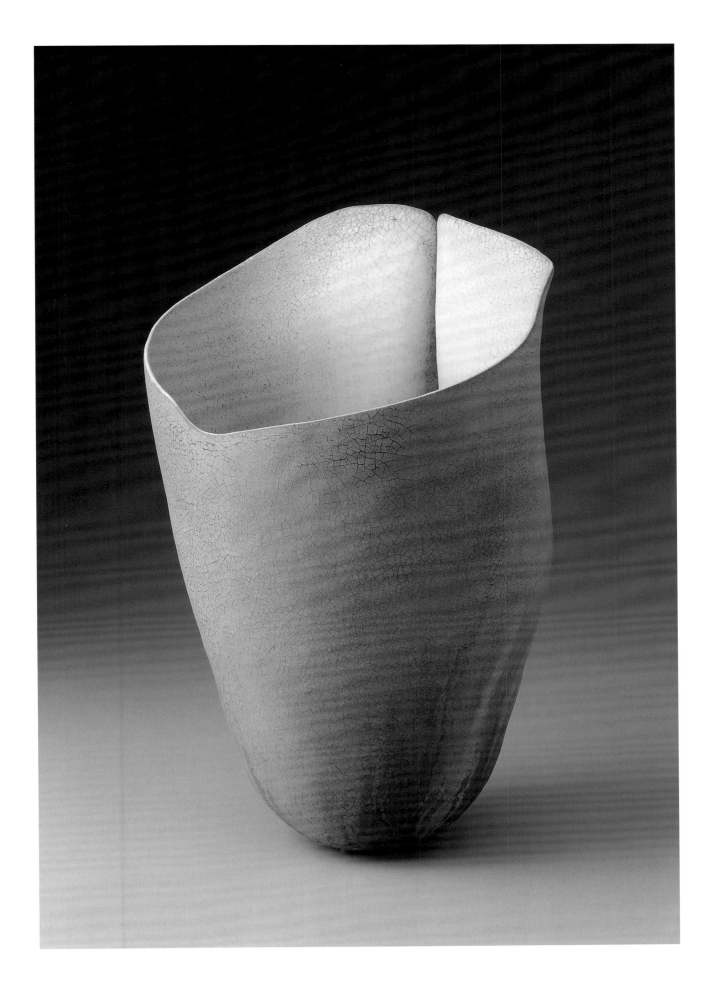

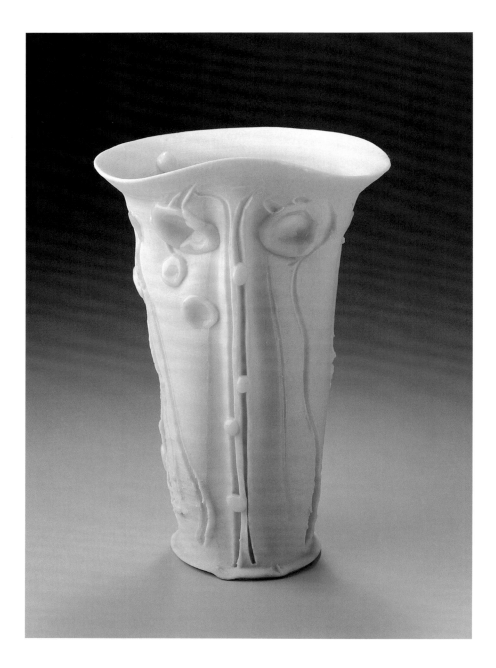

RUDOLF STAFFEL

Light Gatherer, 1985

Porcelain and applied vitreous elements, 7¼ × 5 × 4⅝ in.

JAMES RICHARD DILLINGHAM

Untitled, 1984

Raku-fired glazed earthenware, 9½ × 16 in. diameter

RUTH DUCKWORTH
Untitled (from the *MaMa Pot* series), 1982
Glazed stoneware, 17⅞ × 21 × 19 in.

KEN PRICE

Untitled (Ferro or Block), 1983

Clay and acrylic paint, 4½ × 4½ × 3⅞ in., in wood-
and-glass box construction, 12½ × 12½ × 10½ in.

KEN PRICE

Gunktor, 1985

Fired clay and acrylic paint

Left: 7⅜ × 8¾ × 7¼ in.

Right: 6¾ × 6 × 6 in.

Ken Price

Colors, 1997

Clay and acrylic paint, 18¼ × 12½ × 12½ in.

Karen Karnes

Untitled, 1991

Glazed stoneware and oxides, 11¾ × 17 × 14¼ in.

RON NAGLE

Red and Turquoise Knob Job, 1984
Glazed earthenware, 2⅞ × 4¼ × 2¼ in., in a
painted-wood box construction, 18 × 18 × 5¼ in.

MICHAEL LUCERO
Self-Portrait (Pre-Columbus), 1990
Glazed earthenware, 19⅛ × 11¾ × 11 in.

Michael Lucero
Blue Heart Desert Arch, 1989
Glazed earthenware, 94½ × 13 × 10¾ in.,
on a steel base, ½ × 22¹⁄₁₆ × 14¹⁄₁₆ in.

STEPHEN DE STAEBLER

Pointing Figure Column, 1985
Stoneware, porcelain, and oxides,
96 × 15¼ × 21 in.

Edward S. Eberle

Where the Sky Meets the Ground, 1994

Porcelain and oxides, 13 × 13 × 13 in.

WAYNE HIGBY

Rapids Canyon, 1984–85
Glazed earthenware, 12 × 30 × 16⅞ in.
A. 8 × 11½ × 12 in.; B. 10¾ × 9 × 11 in.; C. 12 × 9 × 9 in.;
D. 11¹³⁄₁₆ × 7¼ × 10 in.

WAYNE HIGBY

Fire Rocks Channel #6, 1982

Glazed earthenware, 11⅛ × 18¼ × 15¼ in.

TOM RIPPON

That's Your Father, 1984
Glazed porcelain, acrylic paint, and pencil, 12¾ × 16 × 14 in.

GEORGES JEANCLOS

Couple Dormeur, 1992
Porcelain and oxides, 9½ × 17¾ × 9 in.

JACK EARL

There Was a Man Afloat in Days, Believing Wisdom Comes with Time, 1983
Glazed earthenware and oil paint, 15½ × 21 × 19½ in.

LIDYA BUZIO

Untitled, 1982

Glazed earthenware, 11⅛ × 9⅞ × 9⅞ in.

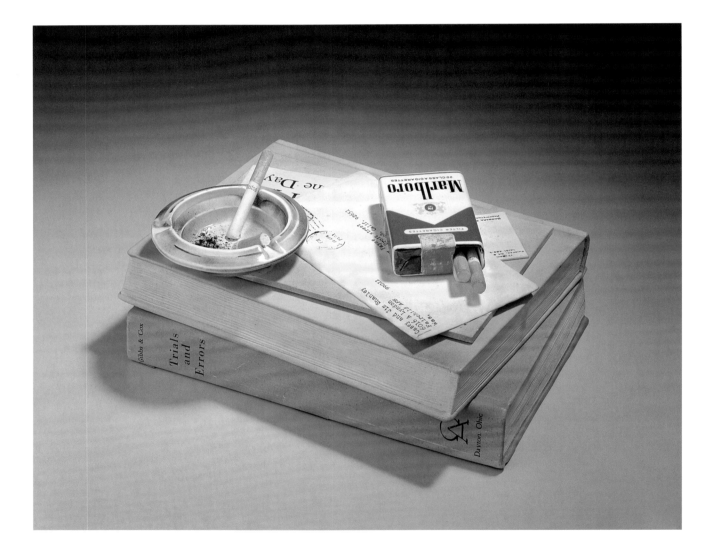

RICHARD SHAW

Book Jar with Ashtray, 1980

Glazed porcelain with decal overglaze, 4¼ × 10 × 7¼ in.

opposite:

VIOLA FREY

Man Observing Series II, 1984

Glazed earthenware, steel, and cement, 106 × 46 × 30 in.

VIOLA FREY

Untitled, 1986

Glazed earthenware, 9 × 25¾ in. diameter

178

ROBERT HUDSON
Teapot, 1973
Porcelain and underglaze,
18⅝ × 10¾ × 6¾ in.

KATHY BUTTERLY

Left: *She Dynasty*, 1998
    Glazed porcelain and earthenware, 5⅛ × 2 in.
Right: *Jiggle*, 1997
    Glazed porcelain, 4½ × 3¼ × 2⅛ in.

BEATRICE WOOD

Large Footed Bowl #63B, 1987

Glazed earthenware, 12½ × 11½ in. diameter

opposite:

RUDY AUTIO

Two Women with a Horse, 1982

Glazed stoneware, 20⅛ × 17¾ × 13⅜ in.

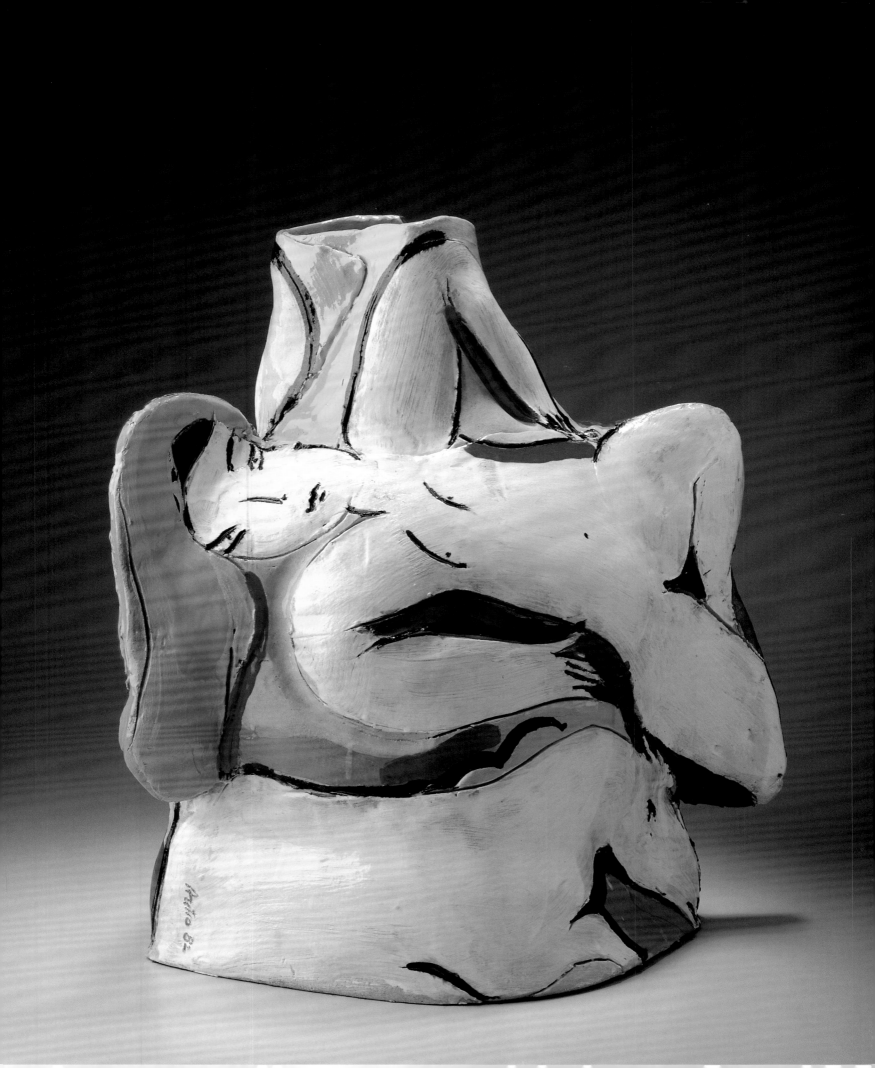

ROBERT ARNESON
Ear Ache, 1991
Glazed earthenware, 15½ × 20 × 7 in.

opposite:
ROBERT ARNESON
A Hollow Jesture, 1971
Glazed earthenware, 20¼ × 12½ × 14 in.

WOOD

opposite:

ALPHONSE MATTIA

Hors d'Oeuvre Server, 1984

Mahogany, walnut, purpleheart, holly, boxwood, poplar, beefwood, ebony, birch, and Baltic birch plywood, 65¾ × 22⅝ × 21¼ in.

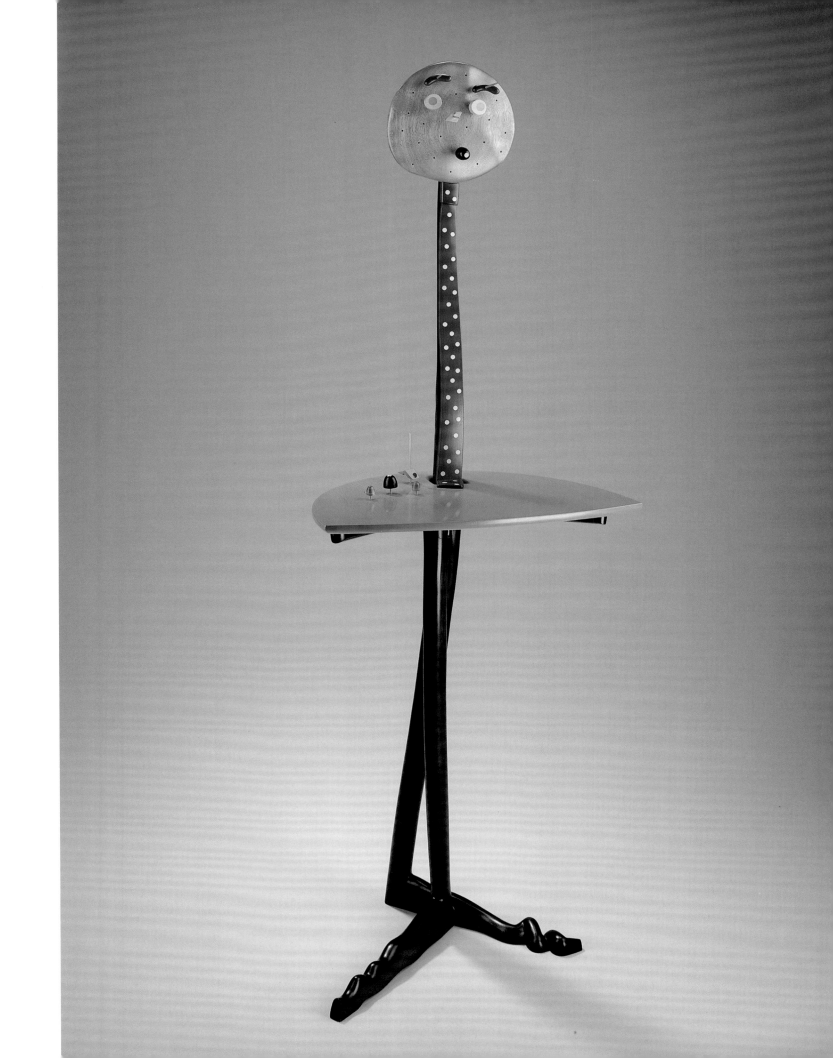

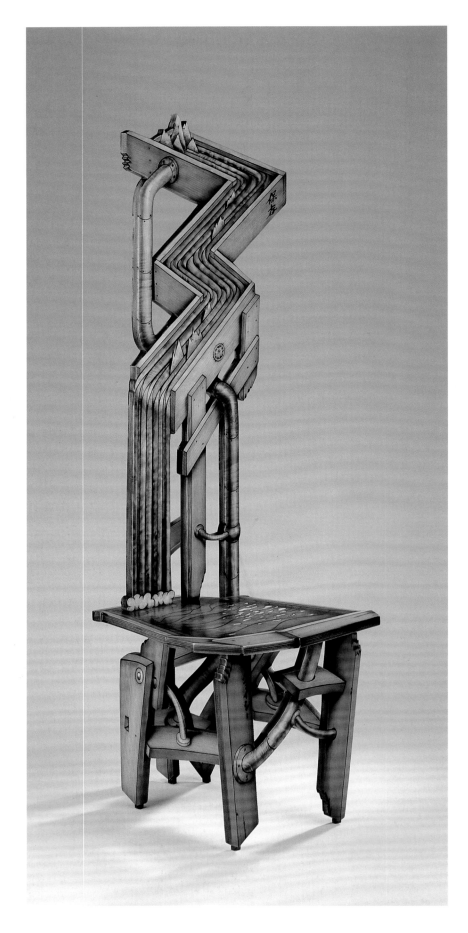

opposite:

JOHN CEDERQUIST

Steamer Chest II, 1994

Baltic birch plywood, ripple maple, poplar, epoxy resin, and lithography inks, 70¼ × 38 × 14⅝ in.

JOHN CEDERQUIST

Conservation Chair, 1998

Baltic birch plywood, Sitka spruce, maple, epoxy resin, aniline dye, and lithography inks, 60½ × 19¾ × 24⅝ in.

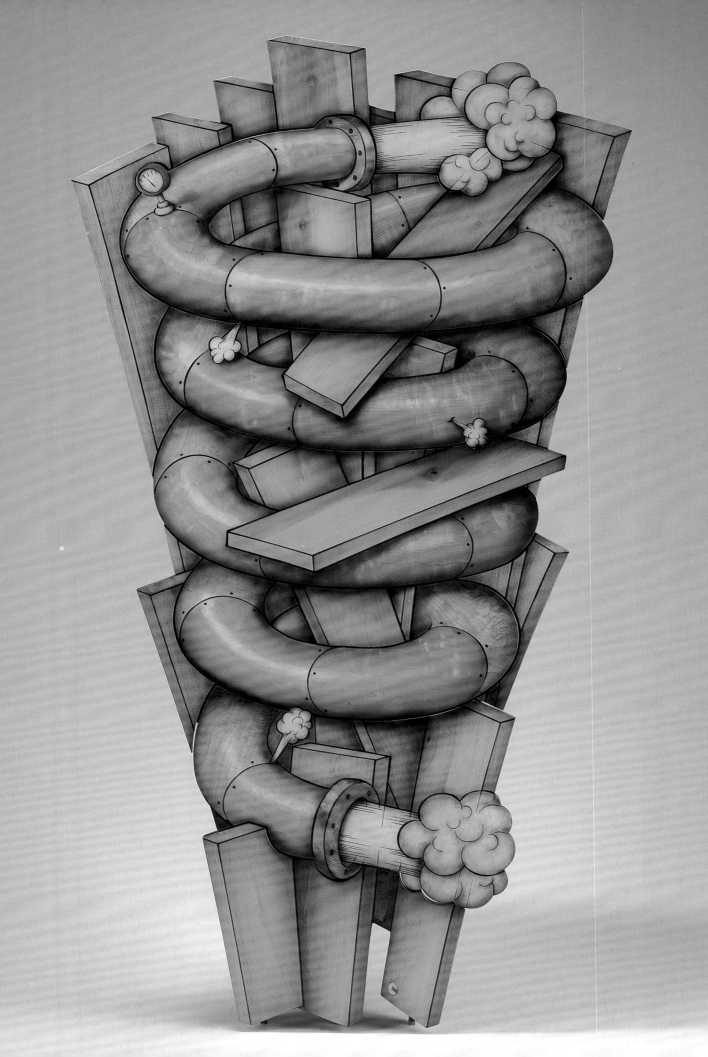

GARRY KNOX BENNETT

Coffee Table, 1982

Yellow satinwood, ebony, plate glass, and pigment,

19¾ × 66 × 26 in.

opposite:

SAM MALOOF
Rocking Chair No. 42, 1994
Ziricote, 44⅛ × 25⅝ × 45⅛ in.

JAY STANGER
Chair, 1986
Bloodwood, curly maple, pearwood, lacewood, pau amarillo,
amaranth, wenge, ebony, and aluminum, 51 × 24¾ × 27¼ in.

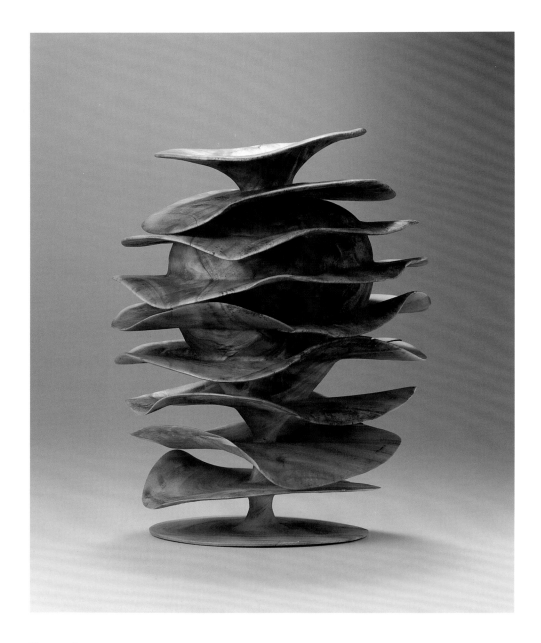

MELVYN FIRMAGER

Seaflower Vessel MF 2-23-C, 1997

Eucalyptus gunnii, 5½ × 4 in. diameter

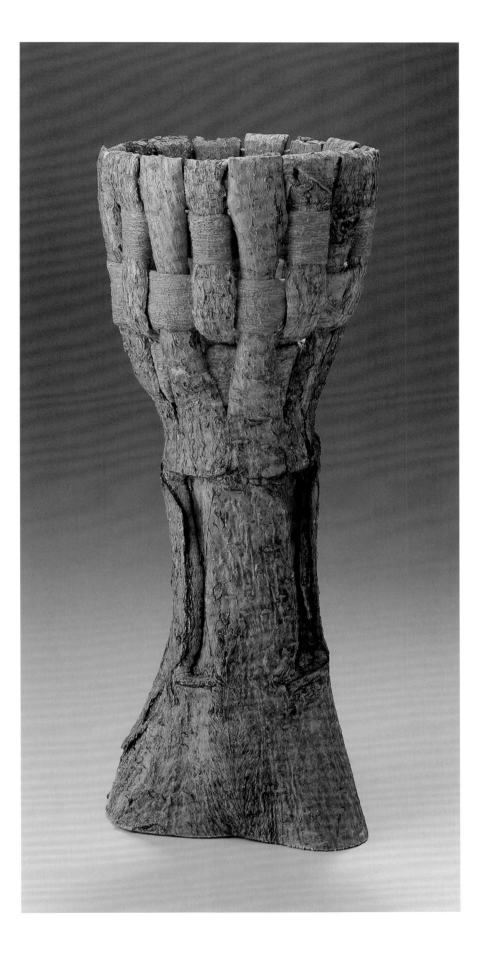

DOROTHY GILL BARNES

Mulberry II (Dendroglyph), 1991–93
Mulberry, 9 × 3½ × 3¼ in.

DEREK BENCOMO

Hula Vessel #4, 1997
Norfolk Island pine, 6¹⁄₁₆ × 5¹⁵⁄₁₆ × 5⁷⁄₈ in.

Derek Bencomo

Paia Valley, Tenth View, 1998

Milo (Hawaii), 3¹⁄₁₆ × 7¾ × 5 in.

MICHAEL JAMES PETERSON

White Coral Bird Vessel, 1996

Bleached and sandblasted locust burl, 3⅛ × 9⅛ × 8⅜ in.

DAVID ELLSWORTH

Pot, 1993
White ash, 4¾ × 6⅞ in. diameter

WILLIAM HUNTER
Zimbabwe Rhythms, 1994
Pink ivory, 3¾ × 6¼ in. diameter

DAN KVITKA

Hollow Vessel #38, 1997

Amboyna, 4½ × 10½ in. diameter

RON FLEMING

Alhambra, 1997

Cocobolo, 6 × 6⅛ in. diameter

207

EDWARD MOULTHROP

White Pine Node Spheroid, 1993
White pine node, 5½ × 7¼ in. diameter

CHRISTIAN BURCHARD

African Blackwood Vessel, 1994

African blackwood, 4¾ × 5 in. diameter

opposite:

MARK LINDQUIST
Captive #9, 1989
Yellow birch burl, 25¾ × 15½ × 22 in.

MARK LINDQUIST
Ascending Bowl #9, 1983
Elm burl, 11½ × 23½ in. diameter

MELVIN LINDQUIST

Maple Burl Vase, 1988

Maple burl, 6½ × 7 in. diameter

opposite:

MELVIN LINDQUIST

Buckeye Root Burl Vase, 1983

Buckeye root burl, 21 × 12½ in. diameter

Michael Shuler

Brazilian Tulipwood Vase, 1997

Brazilian tulipwood, 1⅞ × 4¾ in. diameter

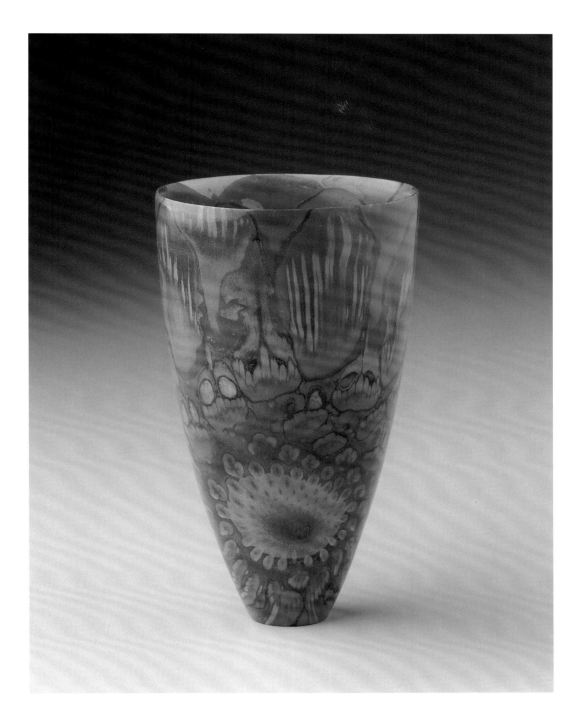

MICHAEL SHULER

Monterey Pinecone Vase, 1997

Monterey pinecone, 3½ × 2¹⁄₁₆ in. diameter

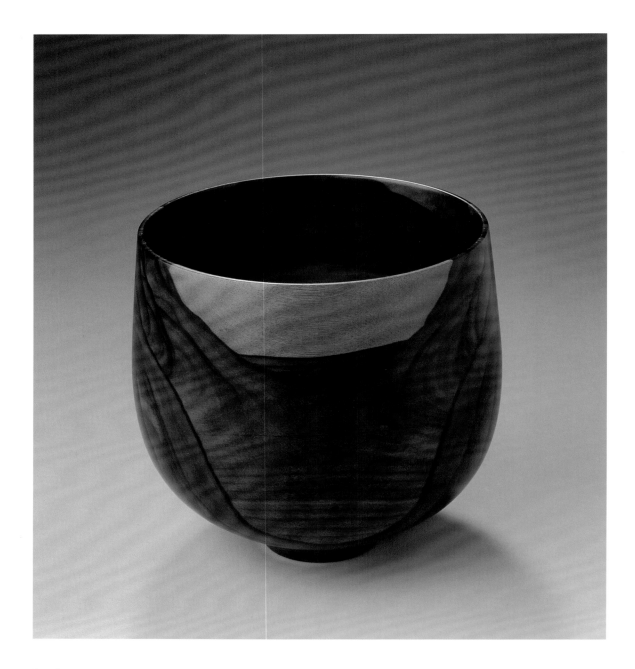

Bob Stocksdale
Ebony Bowl, 1994
Ebony (Malaysia), 5⁵⁄₁₆ × 5⅞ in. diameter

BOB STOCKSDALE

Ziricote Bowl, 1984

Ziricote (Belize), 4⅛ × 6½ in. diameter

BOB STOCKSDALE

Flowering Pear Bowl, 1994

Flowering pear (Berkeley, California), 3⅛ × 5¼ in. diameter

BOB STOCKSDALE

Masur Birch Bowl, 1990

Masur birch (Russia), 3⅞ × 5 × 5 in.

BOB STOCKSDALE

Clockwise from left:

   Kingwood Bowl, 1996

   Kingwood (Brazil), 3⅜ × 5½ × 5¹⁄₁₆ in.

   Pink Ivory Bowl, 1990

   Pink ivory (Zululand), 3½ × 6⁷⁄₁₆ in. diameter

   Pistachio Bowl, 1990

   Pistachio (California), 4⅝ × 7⅞ in. diameter

   Macadamia Bowl, 1991

   Macadamia (Hawaii), 5¼ × 4⅝ × 4½ in.

   Pistachio Bowl, 1996

   Pistachio (California), 5⅛ × 5½ in. diameter

   Magnolia Bowl, 1993

   Magnolia (Texas), 4 × 5½ in. diameter

   Mpingo Bowl, 1996

   Mpingo (Africa), 3⁷⁄₁₆ × 4 × 3½ in.

   Desert Ironwood Bowl, 1982

   Desert ironwood (Arizona), 2½ × 7 in. diameter

   Kingwood Bowl, 1993

   Kingwood (Brazil), 2¹¹⁄₁₆ × 8³⁄₁₆ × 5½ in.

Center left:

   Blackwood Bowl, 1983

   Blackwood (Africa), 3¹⁵⁄₁₆ × 4⅛ in. diameter

Center:

   Texas Mesquite Bowl, 1984

   Mesquite (Texas), 5¼ × 6¼ × 6⅛ in.

Center right:

   Cocobolo Bowl, 1981

   Cocobolo (Mexico), 4 × 5⅛ × 5¼ in.

Vɪᴄ Wᴏᴏᴅ

Untitled Container, 1998

She oak, 2¾ × 6 × 5 in.

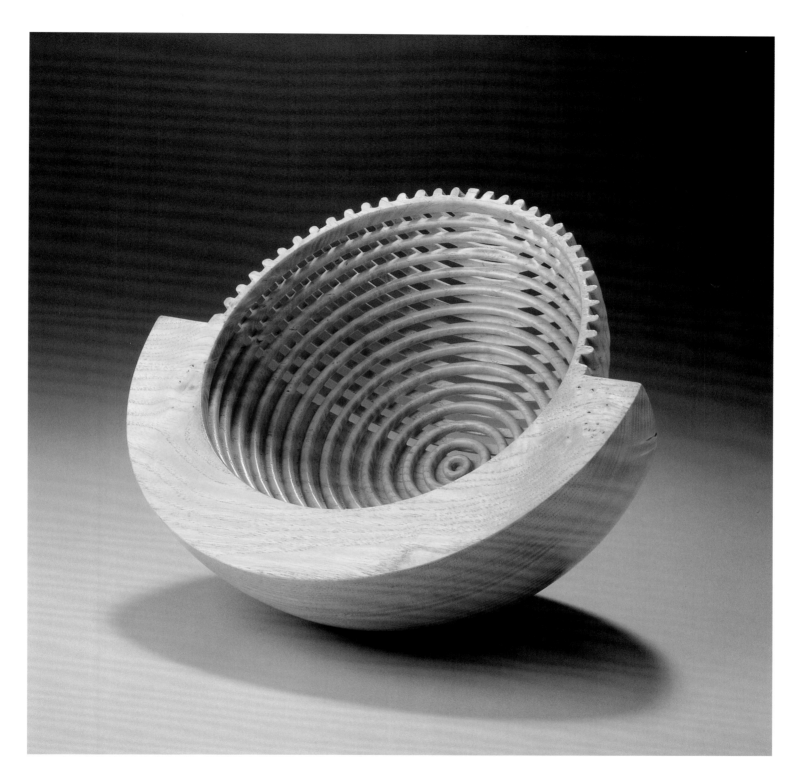

HANS JOACHIM WEISSFLOG
Rocking Bowl, 1998
Ash, 5 × 6½ × 5 in.

FIBER

NEDA AL HILALI

Gate of Gipar, 1986

Acrylic on paper, mounted on canvas, 46 × 91¼ × 1½ in.

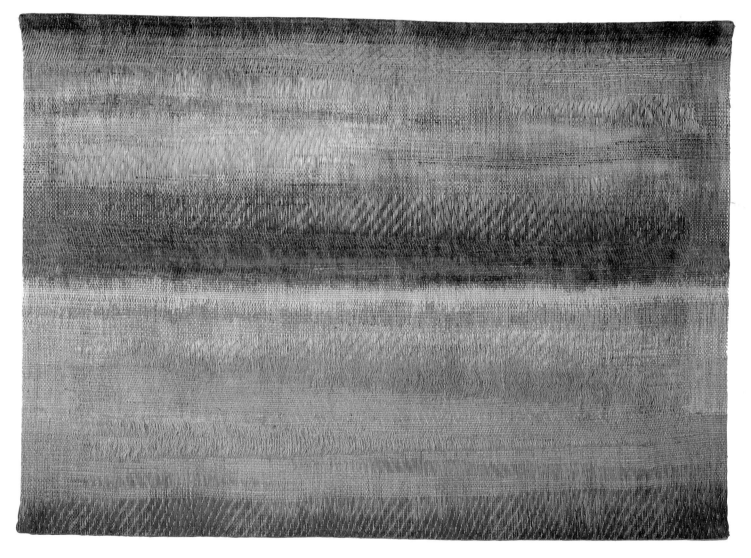

CYNTHIA SCHIRA

Near Balceda, 1984

Cotton, linen, rayon, and mixed fibers, 50 × 65½ × 1 in.

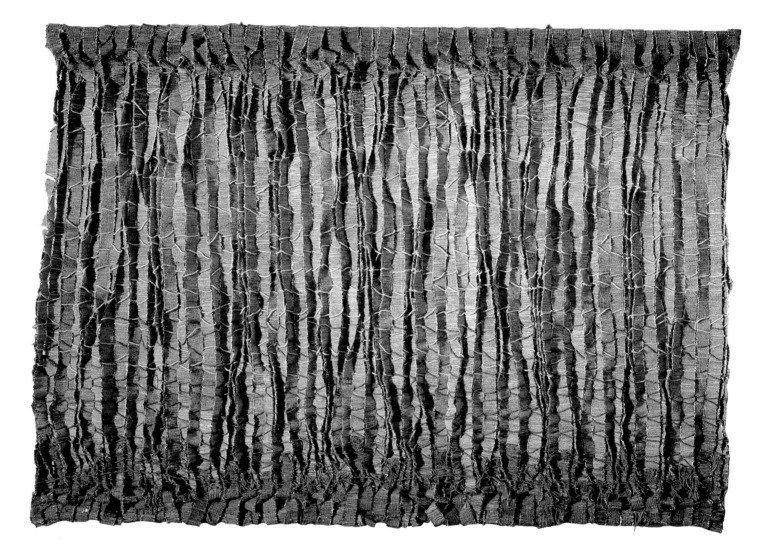

OLGA DE AMARAL

Riscos I (Fibra y Azul), 1983

Wool, linen, horsehair, gesso, and paint, 67 × 88 in.

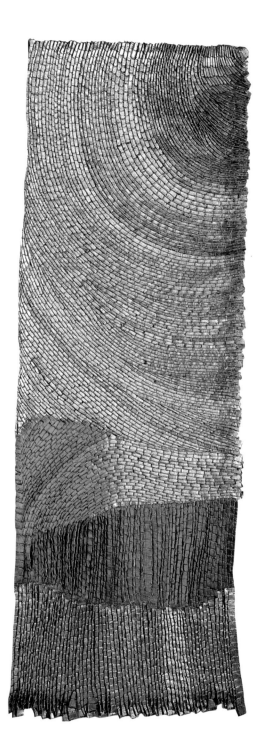

Olga de Amaral

Umbra 5, 1996
Cotton, linen, silver leaf, and acrylic,
mounted on wood, 62 × 21 × ½ in.

LIA COOK

Backstage Curtain, 1984

Rayon, gesso, dyes, and acrylic paint, mounted on board,

60 × 42 × ⅛ in.

LIA COOK

Shadow Frieze, 1990

Rayon, abaca, and dyes, 48⅝ × 69⅜ in.

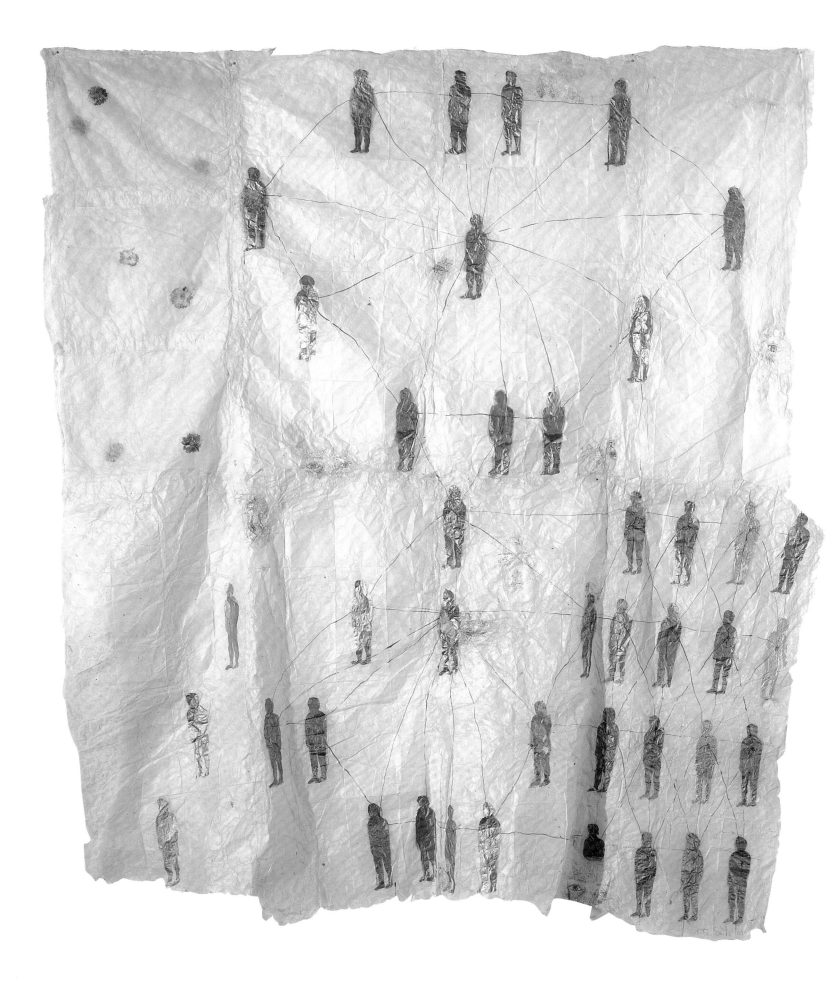

DOMINIC DI MARE

Domus #5—Portochiari, 1983
Wood, horsehair, paint, photograph,
and glass, 45 × 13 × 5 in.

opposite:

KIKI SMITH

Untitled, 1993

Silkscreen, ink, and gold leaf on Nepal
paper and Thai tissue, 75 × 80 in.

DIANE ITTER

Bandana Split #3, 1985
Linen, 17 × 10 in.

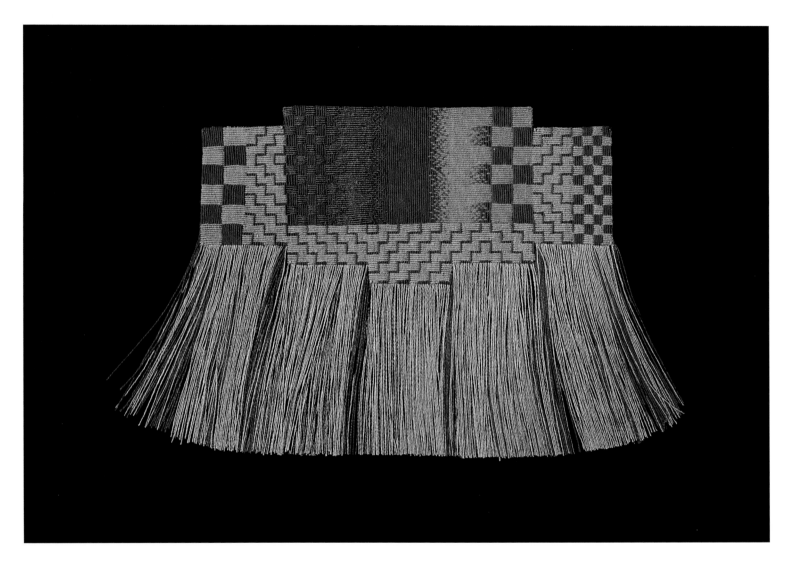

DIANE ITTER

Peruvian Fields, 1985

Linen, 8⅞ × 14 in.

KATHERINE WESTPHAL

Siegrone, 1984

Mylar and metal hands, 6½ × 7½ × 6¾ in.

KARYL SISSON

Hair Receiver, 1995

Cloth tape measures and buttons, 4⅛ × 4⅞ in. diameter

FERNE JACOBS

Head, 1992

Waxed linen thread, 11½ × 16½ × 10¾ in.

PATTI LECHMAN

Left: *Crescendo,* 1992
   Knotted nylon, 6 × 5¾ × 4⅜ in.
Right: *Nataraja,* 1992
   Knotted nylon, 6½ × 5 × 3½ in.

Mary Giles
Men's Stele, 1993
Waxed linen, 10 × 8 × 2¾ in.

opposite:
Jane Sauer
Devouring the Earth, 1992
Thread and paint
Left: 16⅞ × 3¾ × 3¼ in.
Right: 4¼ × 3⅜ × 3¾ in.

CAROL ECKERT

Swan Maidens, 1997

Cotton thread and wire, 7⅜ × 10½ × 4½ in.

JEANNINE ANDERSON

Three Forms, 1994
Glass beads and thread, 3¾ × 6¾ × 3¼ in.

Untitled, 1982

Japanese handmade paper and linen thread, 3¾ × 7½ in. diameter

KAY SEKIMACHI

Untitled, 1994

Antique Japanese paper and linen, 3¼ × 5⅞ in. diameter

KAY SEKIMACHI

Left: *Leaf Vessel XXIV*, 1997
    Big-leaf maple leaves and paper, 4⅞ × 4¾ in.
    diameter

Right: *Leaf Vessel XXV*, 1997
    Big-leaf maple leaves and paper, 6⅞ × 5¼ in.
    diameter

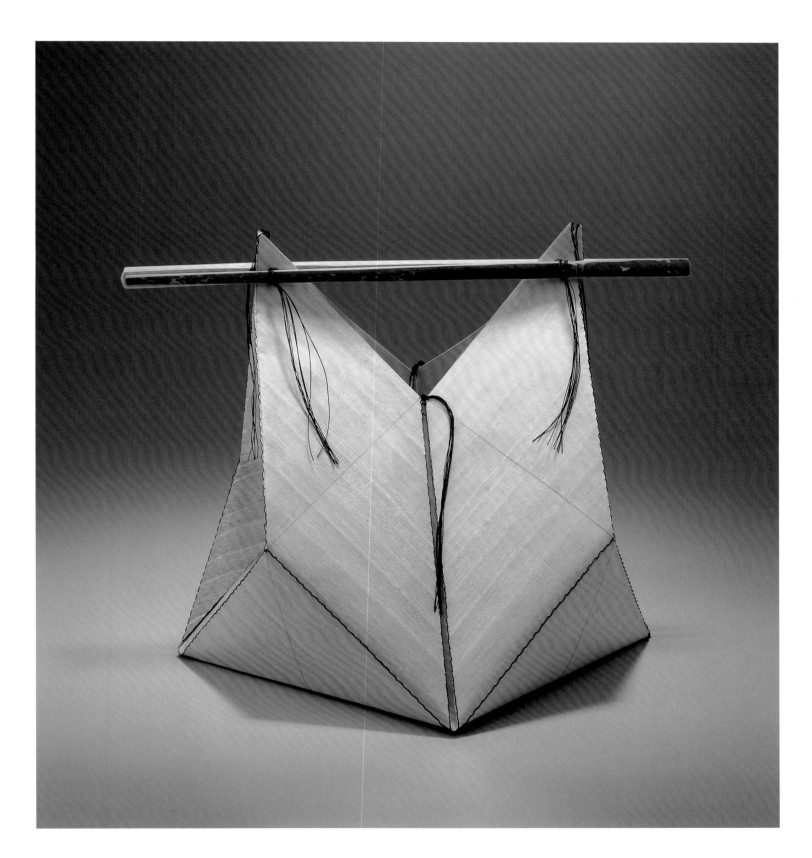

KAY SEKIMACHI

KIRI II (#11), 1993

Kiriwood paper, silk tissue, and black bamboo handles, 7½ × 9⅞ × 8⅛ in.

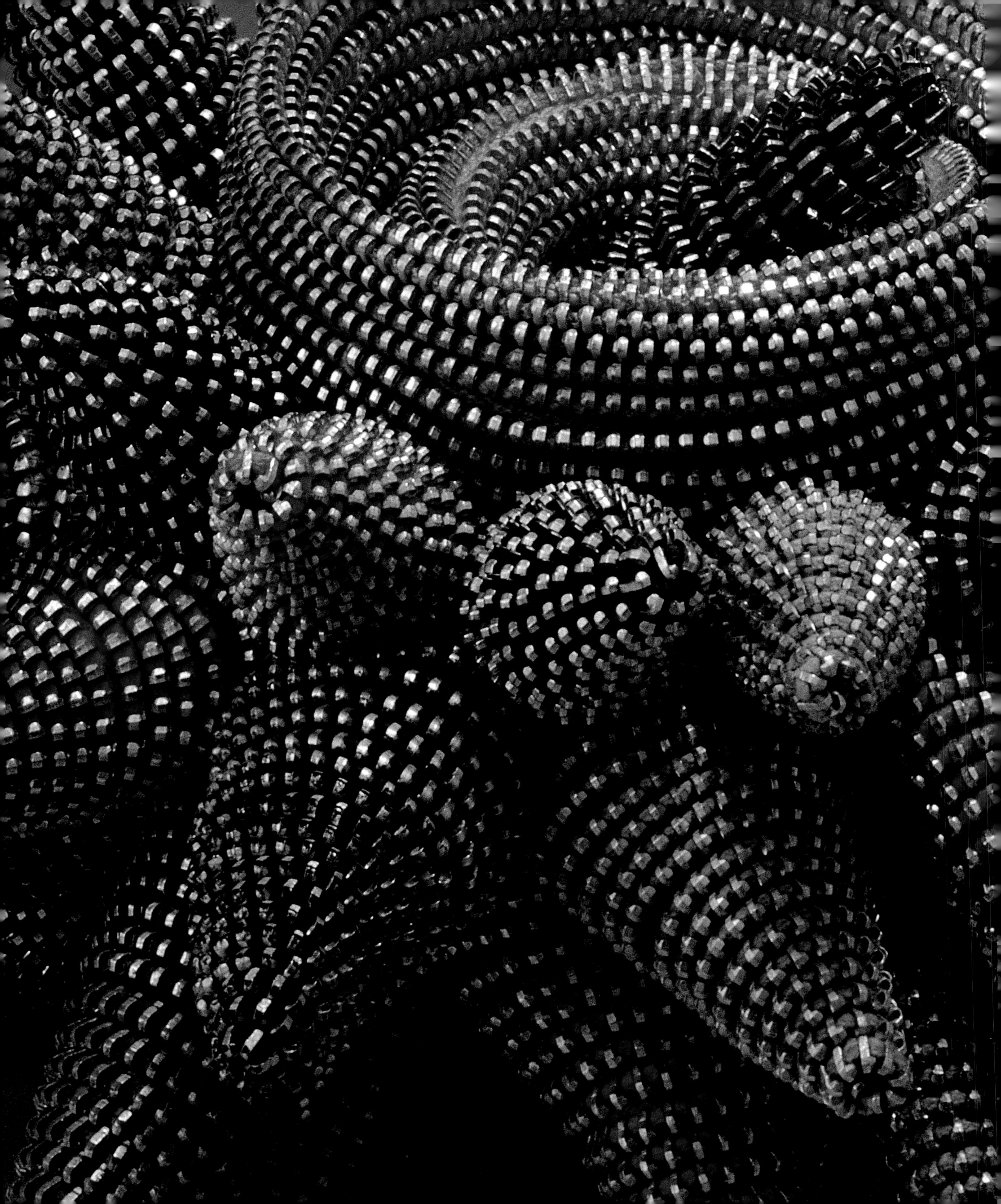

METAL

opposite:

Richard Deutsch

Journey, 1997

Bronze, 33 × 36 × 8¼ in.

JUNE SCHWARCZ

Raku Vessel, 1981
Electroplated copper foil with raku enameling, 7 × 6⅜ in. diameter

SUSAN COLQUITT

Vespertine, 1992

Aluminum zippers and cotton, 5½ × 7½ × 7½ in.

JUDY KENSLEY McKIE
Jaguar Bench, 1993
Bronze, 26½ × 58½ × 17½ in.

MANUEL NERI

Untitled, 1981–83

Bronze and enamel paint, 58⅝ × 17¾ ×
16 in. (with contiguous base)

SELECTED BIBLIOGRAPHY

opposite:

MANUEL NERI

Maquette II, 1988

Plaster, wood, and dry pigments, 19½ × 11⅛ × 10⅞ in.

THE SAXE COLLECTION

Approaches to Collecting: Profiles of Recent Private and Corporate Collections. New York: American Craft Museum, 1982.

Clowes, Jody. "Toledo Museum of Art." *American Craft* 54 (April/May 1994): 38–43.

Contemporary American and European Glass from the Saxe Collection, exh. cat. Essays by Kenneth R. Trapp and William Warmus. Oakland: The Oakland Museum, 1986.

Kelhman, Robert. "Glass of the '80s: Collectors George and Dorothy Saxe Document a Decade." *American Craft* 47, no. 2 (April/May 1987): 32–39.

Knoerle, Jane. "The Saxes' Hobby Has Grown into a World Class Collection." *The Country Almanac* , 3 April 1991, Home and Garden Special Section.

Lynn, Vanessa S. "The Art of Collecting." *American Ceramics* 7, no. 2 (1988): 12.

Malarcher, Patricia. "The Saxe Collection Contemporary American and European Glass." *Craft International* 6 (July/September 1987): 28.

Martin, Loy. "Embedded Energies: Reflections on the George and Dorothy Saxe Collection." *Furniture Studio One.* Newtown, Conn.: Cambium Press, 1999.

Morris, Gay. "Peninsula Husband and Wife Discover New World through Sculpture in Glass." *Peninsula Times Tribune,* 17 September 1982.

Nicola, Günter. "American and European Glass from the Saxe Collection." *Neues Glas* 3 (July/September 1987): 214–15.

Pacheco, Patrick, ed. "America's Top 100 Collectors." *Art & Antiques* 17 (March 1994): 94.

———, ed. "The 100 Top Collectors in America." *Art & Antiques* 19 (March 1996): 95.

Rosen, Laura. "Capitol Crafts: The Saxe Collection Ends Its National Tour at the Smithsonian's Renwick Gallery." *American Style* (Fall 1994/Winter 1995): 36–41.

S., L. C. "Classics: Looking at the 21st Century. Collecting the Latest." *San Francisco Chronicle,* 28 October 1992.

Saxe, Dorothy. "'I Can't Hug a Painting' . . . How an Introduction to the World of Studio Craft Changed the Lives of Well-Known Collectors George and Dorothy Saxe." *The Crafts Report* 24 (February 1998): 20–23.

Taragin, Davira S. *Contemporary Crafts and the Saxe Collection*, exh. cat. Toledo: Toledo Museum of Art in association with Hudson Hills Press, New York, 1993.

———. "Selections from the George and Dorothy Saxe Collection at the Toledo Museum of Art." *Glass Art Society Journal* (1993): 129–30.

"The Saxe Collection in New York City." *Neues Glas* 2 (1987): 105.

Page numbers in italic refer to illustrations of work.

HANK MURTA ADAMS
Born 1956, Philadelphia, Pennsylvania
p. 107
Perspectives: Hank Murta Adams, exh. brochure. Sheboygan, Mich.: John Michael Kohler Arts Center, 1988.
Sculpture: Hank Murta Adams, exh. cat. Cullowhee, N.C.: Chelsea Gallery, Hinds University Center, Western Carolina University, 1986.

NICOLAS AFRICANO
Born 1948, Kankakee, Illinois
p. 108
Nicolas Africano: Two Sisters. Essay by Lisa Lyons. Seattle: Meyerson & Nowinski Art Associates, 1997.
Reed, Dupuy Warrick. "Nicolas Africano: Responsible Relevance." *Arts Magazine* 53 (June 1979): 158–60.
Shannon, Mark. "Nicolas Africano: A Performing Art." *Art Space* (March/ April 1990): 56–57.

NEDA AL HILALI
Born 1938, Cheb, Czechoslovakia
p. 224
Neda Al Hilali, exh. cat. Text by Sandy Ballatore. Los Angeles: Los Angeles Municipal Art Society, 1985.
"Neda Al Hilali: An Interview by Betty Park." *Fiberarts* 6, no. 4 (July– August 1979): 40–45.
Manhart, Marcia, and Tom Manhart, eds. *The Eloquent Object: The Evolution of American Art in Craft Media since 1945*. Tulsa, Okla.: Philbrook Museum of Art, 1987.

JEANNINE ANDERSON
Born 1956, Chicago, Illinois
p. 243
Contemporary Beadwork: Innovative Directions, exh. cat. Loveland, Colo.: Loveland Museum/Gallery, 1995.
Fiberart Design Book Five. Asheville, N.C.: Lark Books, 1995.
"New Baskets: A Portfolio." *Fiberarts* 19 (Summer 1990): 16–21.

ROBERT ARNESON
Born 1930, Benicia, California; died 1992
pp. 185–187
Benezra, Neal. *Robert Arneson: A Retrospective*, exh. cat. Des Moines, Iowa: Des Moines Art Center, 1985.
Robert Arneson: Self-Portraits, exh. cat. Philadephia: Moore College of Art, 1979.

Robert Arneson: Self-Reflection, exh. cat. San Francisco: San Francisco Museum of Modern Art, 1997.

RUDY AUTIO
Born 1926, Butte, Montana
p. 183
Autio, Lela, and Lar Autio. *Rudy Autio: Work, 1983–1996*. Missoula, Mont.: White Swan Press, 1996.
Lebow, Edward. "The Fleshpots of Rudy Autio." *American Ceramics* 4, no. 1 (1985): 32–37.
Rudy Autio: A Retrospective, exh. cat. Text by Matthew Kangas, James G. Todd, and Ted Waddell. Missoula: University of Montana, School of Fine Arts, 1983.

RALPH BACERRA
Born 1938, Garden Grove, California
pp. 148–149
Clark, Garth. *American Ceramics: 1876 to the Present*. New York: Abbeville Press, 1987.
Lauria, Jo. "Ralph Bacerra—Ceramic Artist." *Ceramics: Art and Perception* 15 (1994): 15–19.
McCloud, Mac. "Deliberately Decorative: The Ceramics of Ralph Bacerra." *American Craft* 47 (June/July 1987): 50–55.

DOROTHY GILL BARNES
Born 1927, Strawberry Point, Iowa
p. 199
Dorothy Gill Barnes/John Garrett, exh. cat. Winton, Conn.: Brown/Grotta Gallery, 1996.
Janeiro, Jan. "Drawing on Trees: Dorothy Gill Barnes." *American Craft* 56 (February/March 1996): 44–47.
Keen, Annette. "Dorothy Barnes Fantasy Baskets." *Shuttle, Spindle & Dyepot* 19 (Spring 1988): 22–24.

BENNETT BEAN
Born 1941, Cincinnati, Ohio
p. 152
Busch, Akiko. "Bennett Bean." *American Craft* 48, no. 2 (April/May 1988): 24–29.
Chambers, Karen. "Bennett Bean: Playing by His Rules." *Ceramic Monthly* 46 (March 1998): 43–46.
Leaning into the Wind: Ceramic Works by Bennett Bean, exh. cat. Little Rock: Arkansas Art Center, Decorative Arts Museum, 1996.

LARRY BELL
Born 1939, Chicago, Illinois
p. 59
Larry Bell: Major Works in Glass, exh. cat. Lincoln: Sheldon Memorial Art Gallery, University of Nebraska, 1983.
Wortz, Melinda. "Larry Bell." *Glass Art Society Journal* (1986): 58–61.
Zones of Experience: The Art of Larry Bell, exh. cat. Albuquerque, N.M.: Albuquerque Museum, 1997.

DEREK BENCOMO

Born 1962, Torrance, California

pp. 200–201

Expressions in Wood: Masterworks from the Wornick Collection, exh. cat. Essays by Matthew Kangas, John Perreault, Edward S. Cooke, Jr., and Tran Turner. Oakland: Oakland Museum of California in association with University of Washington Press, Seattle, 1996.

LYNDA BENGLIS

Born 1941, Lake Charles, Louisiana

p. 106

Krane, Susan. *Lynda Benglis: Dual Natures*, exh. cat. Atlanta: High Museum of Art in association with University of Washington Press, Seattle, 1990.

Lynda Benglis: Works in Glass. Los Angeles: Margo Leavin Gallery, 1985.

Ratcliff, Carter. *Lynda Benglis, Keith Sonnier: A Ten-Year Retrospective, 1977–1987*, exh. cat. Alexandria, La: Alexandria Museum of Art, 1987.

GARRY KNOX BENNETT

Born 1934, Alameda, California

p. 195

Cooke, Edward S., Jr. *New American Furniture: The Second Generation of Studio Furnituremakers*, exh. cat. Boston: Museum of Fine Arts, 1989.

Kelsey, John. "Portfolio: Garry Knox Bennett." *Fine Woodworking* 45 (March/April 1984): 79–81.

Stone, Michael. "Garry Knox Bennett." *American Craft* 44, no. 5 (October/ November 1984): 22–26.

HOWARD BEN TRÉ

Born 1949, Brooklyn, New York

pp. 102–105

Howard Ben Tré: New Work. Interview by Diana Johnson, essay by Donald Kuspit. Providence, R.I.: Brown University, 1993.

Howard Ben Tré: Recent Sculpture, exh. cat. Text by Richard Waller and Gary Sangster. Richmond, Va.: Marsh Art Gallery, University of Richmond in association with Cleveland Center for Contemporary Art, Ohio, 1996.

Johnson, Linda L. *Howard Ben Tré. Contemporary Sculpture*, exh. cat. Washington, D.C.: The Phillips Collection, 1989.

CHRISTINA BERTONI

Born 1945, Ann Arbor, Michigan

p. 143

Cobb, James. "Christina Bertoni." *American Ceramics* 6, no. 3 (1988): 30–37.

Tarlow, Lois. "Christina Bertoni." *Art New England* 5, no. 5 (April 1984): 8.

Wechsler, Susan. "Celestial Bodies." *American Ceramics* 2 (February 1983): 22–25.

ZOLTÁN BOHUS

Born 1941, Endröd, Hungary

p. 50

Lugossy, Maria, and Zoltán Bohus. "Glass in Hungary/Hungarians in Glass." *Glass Art Society Journal* (1997): 38–39.

Maria Lugossy, Zoltán Bohus. Text by Janos Frank. Fellbach, Austria: Stadt Fellbach, Druckerei Schwertschlag Fellbach, 1987.

"Vertiges" Maria Lugossy—Zoltán Bohus, exh. cat. Paris: Galerie d'Amon, 1986.

JAROSLAVA BRYCHTOVÁ

Jaroslava Brychtová, born 1924, Železný Brod, Czechoslovakia

pp. 100–102

Museum Bellerive, Zurich. *Skulpturen aus Glas: Stanislav Libenský und Jaroslava Brychtová, Prag Eine Retrospektive 1945–1990.* Text by Sigrid Barten, Ludmila Vachtová, Sylva Petrová, Jaroslava Brychtová, and Stanislav Libenský. Zurich, 1990.

Stanislav Libenský/Jaroslava Brychtová: A 40-year Collaboration in Glass, exh. cat. Edited by Susanne K. Frantz with contributions by Thomas S. Buechner, Susanne K. Frantz, Sylva Petrová, and Jiří Setlik. Corning, N.Y.: The Corning Museum of Glass; Munich: Prestel, 1994.

Vašíček, Aleš. "An Interview with Stanislav Libenský and Jaroslava Brychtová." *Glasswork* 10 (October 1991): 10–19.

CHRISTIAN BURCHARD

Born 1955, Hamburg, Germany

p. 209

Expressions in Wood: Masterworks from the Wornick Collection, exh. cat. Essays by Matthew Kangas, John Perreault, Edward S. Cooke, Jr., and Tran Turner. Oakland: Oakland Museum of California in association with University of Washington Press, Seattle, 1996.

Nolte, Martin. "Der Ausdruck Zämlt." *Das Dreckseln* 3 (1998): 10–14.

"Portfolio." *American Craft* 51 (October/November 1991): 52–62.

KATHY BUTTERLY

Born 1963, Amityville, New York

p. 181

Adkins, Gretchen. "The Pots of Kathy Butterly." *Ceramics: Art and Perception*, no. 23 (1996): 29–31.

Chambers, Karen S. "Kathy Butterly." *American Ceramics* 12, no. 2 (1996): 50.

Glueck, Grace. "Kathy Butterfly." *New York Times*, 10 October 1998.

LIDYA BUZIO

Born 1948, Montevideo, Uruguay

p. 175

Buzio, Lydia. "Line and Rhythm." *Studio Potter* 14 (December 1985): 44.

Lebow, Edward. "Lidya Buzio: In Perspective." *American Ceramics* 2, no. 2 (1983): 34–39.

WILLIAM CARLSON

Born 1950, Dover, Ohio

p. 60

Carlson/Weinberg, exh. cat. Boca Raton, Fla.: Habatat Galleries, 1990.

William Carlson, exh. cat. Text by James Yood. Chicago: Marx-Saunders Gallery, 1996.

Zerwick, Chloe. "William Carlson: Balanced Asymmetry." *American Craft* 42, no. 3 (June–July 1982): 2–5.

WENDELL CASTLE

Born 1932, Emporia, Kansas

p. 194

Masterworks, exh. cat. Essays by Peter T. Joseph, Witold Rybczynski, and Arthur C. Danto. New York: Peter Joseph Gallery, 1991.

Taragin, Davira Spiro. *Furniture by Wendell Castle.* New York: Hudson Hill Press in association with Founders Society, Detroit Institute of Arts, 1989.

Wendell Castle Picture Tables, exh. cat. New York: Peter Joseph Gallery, 1992.

JOHN CEDERQUIST

Born 1946, Altadena, California

pp. 192–193

Cooke, Edward S., Jr. " John Cederquist: Le Fleuron Manquant." *New American Furniture: The Second Generation of Studio Furnituremakers*, exh. cat. Boston: Franklin Graphics, 1989.

Danto, Arthur, and Nancy Princenthal. *The Art of John Cederquist: Reality of Illusion*, exh. cat. Introduction by Kenneth R. Trapp. Oakland: Oakland Museum of California, 1997.

Emanuelli, Sharon K. "John Cederquist: Deception." *American Craft* 43, no. 5 (October/November 1983): 24–27.

DALE CHIHULY

Born 1941, Tacoma, Washington

pp. 66–68 (detail), 69–75, 129

Bannard, Walter Darby, and Henry Geldzahler. *Chihuly: Form from Fire*, exh. cat. Daytona Beach, Fla.: The Museum of Arts and Sciences, 1993.

Chihuly, Dale. *Chihuly: Color, Glass, and Form.* Tokyo and New York: Kodansha International Ltd., 1986.

Kuspit, Donald B. *Chihuly.* Introduction by Jack Cowart. 2nd ed. New York: Harry N. Abrams; Seattle: Portland Press, 1998.

DANIEL CLAYMAN

Born 1957, Lynn, Massachusetts

p. 112

Luecking, Stephen. Betsy Rosenfeld Gallery, Chicago, exhibit. *American Craft* 54 (April/May 1994): 90.

SUSAN COLQUITT

Born 1955, Detroit, Michigan

pp. 248 (detail), 253

Fiberarts Design Book Five. Asheville, N.C.: Lark Books, 1995.

Nouvel Object III. Seoul, Korea: Design House Publications, 1997.

"Portfolio: Susie Colquitt." *American Craft* 74, no. 4 (August/September 1998): 74.

LIA COOK

Born 1942, Ventura, California

pp. 222 (detail), 228–229

Alexander, Judy. "Lia Cook: Exploring the Territory Where Painting and Textiles Meet." *Fiberarts* 9 (September/October 1982): 28–31.

Brooks-Myers, Inez, et al. *Lia Cook: Material Allusions*, exh. cat. Oakland: Oakland Museum of California, 1995.

Conner, Maureen. "The Tapestries of Lia Cook." *Arts Magazine* 59, no. 6 (February 1985): 94–95.

DAN DAILEY

Born 1947, Philadephia, Pennsylvania

pp. 116, 117, frontispiece

Chambers, Karen. "Dan Dailey: A Designing Character." *Neues Glas* 1 (1990): 10–19.

Dan Dailey: Simple Complexities in Drawings and Glass, 1972–1987, exh. cat. Philadelphia: Philadelphia Colleges of the Arts, 1987.

Matano, Koji. "Dan Dailey." Interview by author. *Glasswork* 6 (August 1990): 12–19.

OLGA de AMARAL

Born 1932, Bogotá, Colombia

pp. 226–227

Olga de Amaral: Lost Images, Inherited Landscapes, exh. cat. Text by Mildred Constantine. Overland Park, Kans.: Johnson County Community College, Gallery of Art, 1992.

Olga de Amaral: Nine Stelae and Other Landscapes, exh. cat. Curated by Pilar Jacquelin. Fresno, Calif.: The Fresno Art Museum, 1996.

Talley, Charles. "Olga de Amaral." *American Craft* 48, no. 2 (April/May 1988): 38–45.

STEPHEN DE STAEBLER

Born 1933, Saint Louis, Missouri

p. 167

Ashton, Dore. "Objects Worked by the Imagination for Their Innerness: The Sculpture of Stephen De Staebler." *Arts Magazine* 59 (November 1984): 140–44.

Lindberg, Ted. *Stephen De Staebler*, exh. cat. Vancouver: Emily Carr College of Art and Design; San Francisco: The Art Museum Association of America, 1983.

Stephen De Staebler: The Figure, exh. cat. Essay by Donald Kuspit. San Francisco: Chronicle Books; Laguna Beach, Calif.: Laguna Art Museum, Saddleback College, 1987.

RICHARD DEUTSCH

Born 1953, Los Angeles, California

p. 251

Clark, Garth. *American Ceramics: 1876 to the Present.* New York: Abbeville Press, 1987.

Misrach, Myriam Weisang. "Ideas beneath the Surface." *The Museum of California* 17 (Winter 1993): 9.

Voyage: From Ship's Propellor to Sculpture. Oakland: Branalea Pacific, 1991.

RICHARD DEVORE

Born 1933, Toledo, Ohio

pp. 130 (detail), 153

Dunas, Richard, and Sarah Bodine. "Richard DeVore: The Myth of Fingerprints." *American Ceramics* 7, no. 4 (1989): 18–27.

Richard DeVore 1972–1982, exh. cat. Milwaukee, Wis.: Milwaukee Art Museum, 1983.

Rubenfeld, Florence. "The Pottery of Richard DeVore." *American Craft* 43, no. 5 (October/November 1983): 34–38.

JAMES RICHARD DILLINGHAM

Born 1952, Lake Forest, Illinois; died 1994

p. 156

Kane, Sid. "Patchwork Pots." *American Craft* 41, no. 5 (October/November 1981): 36–39.

Kangas, Matthew. "Rick Dillingham and the Reparative Drive." *American Ceramics* 8, no. 4 (1990): 26–35.

Rick Dillingham, exh. cat. Santa Fe, N.M.: Linda Durham Gallery, 1990.

DOMINIC DI MARE

Born 1932, San Francisco, California

p. 231

Janeiro, Jan. "Dominic Di Mare: 'The Shore Is the Magical Place Where the Water Meets the Land.'" *American Craft* 58 (February/March 1998): 46–51.

Mayfield, Signe. *Dominic Di Mare: A Retrospective,* exh. cat. Palo Alto, Calif.: Palo Alto Cultural Center, 1997.

Park, Betty. "Dominic Di Mare: Houses for the Sacred." *American Craft* 42 (October/November 1982): 2–6.

RUTH DUCKWORTH

Born 1919, Hamburg, Germany

p. 157

McTwigan, Michael. "Ruth Duckworth." *American Ceramics* 10, no. 2 (1992): 18–27.

Ruth Duckworth/Claire Zeisler, exh. cat. Text by Helen Williams Drutt. Philadelphia: Moore College of Art, 1979.

Vanderstappen, Harrie A. "Ruth Duckworth: Life Becomes Sculpture." *American Craft* 51 (October/November 1991): 34–39.

JACK EARL

Born 1934, near Uniopolis, Ohio

p. 174

Klassen, John. "A Conversation with Jack Earl." *Ceramics Monthly* 29, no. 8 (October 1981): 68–70.

Nordness, Lee. *Jack Earl: The Genesis and Triumphant Survival of an Underground Ohio Artist.* Racine, Wis.: Perimeter Press Limited, 1985.

Ohio Boy: The Ceramic Sculpture of Jack Earl, exh. cat. Sheboygan, Wis.: John Michael Kohler Arts Center, 1987.

EDWARD S. EBERLE

Born 1944, Tarentum, Pennsylvania

p. 168

Clark, Vicky. "Artist Project." *American Ceramics* 10, no. 2 (Spring 1994): 44–49.

Koplos, J. "Edward Eberle." *Art in America* 84, no. 5 (May 1996): 114.

CAROL ECKERT

Born 1945, Chapel Hill, North Carolina

p. 242

Brandt, Beverly K. "Carol Eckert: The Power of the Small." *American Craft* 59, no. 2 (April/May 1999): 58–61.

Lineberry, Heather Sealy. "Carol Eckert." *Fiberarts* (Summer 1992): 12.

Shermeta, Margo. "Three Contemporary Basketmakers: Form Dissolved from Function." *Art Today* 5, no. 3 (1990): 30–33.

DAVID ELLSWORTH

Born 1944, Iowa City, Iowa

p. 203

Expressions in Wood: Masterworks from the Wornick Collection, exh. cat. Essays by Matthew Kangas, John Perreault, Edward S. Cooke, Jr., and Tran Turner. Oakland: Oakland Museum of California in association with University of Washington Press, Seattle, 1996.

Raffan, Richard. "Current Work in Turning." *Fine Woodworking,* no. 67 (November/December 1987): 92–95.

Sewell, D. "David Ellsworth." *Bulletin—Philadelphia Museum of Art* 87, no. 371 (Fall 1991): 18–19.

MELVYN FIRMAGER

Born 1944, Walton on Thames, Surrey, England

p. 198

Expressions in Wood: Masterworks from the Wornick Collection, exh. cat. Essays by Matthew Kangas, John Perreault, Edward S. Cooke, Jr., and Tran Turner. Oakland: Oakland Museum of California in association with University of Washington Press, Seattle, 1996.

RON FLEMING

Born 1937, Oklahoma City, Oklahoma

pp. 188 (detail), 206

Hawks, Bob. "Floral Visions: How Ron Fleming Turns and Carves His Bowls." *Fine Woodworking,* no. 99 (March/April 1993): 54–57.

Monroe, Michael W. *The White House Colllection of American Crafts.* Text by Barbaralee Diamonstein, foreword by Elisabeth Broun. New York: Harry N. Abrams, Inc., 1995.

VIOLA FREY

Born 1933, Lodi, California

pp. 178–179

It's All Part of the Clay: Viola Frey, exh. cat. Text by Patterson Sims and interview with Frey by Garth Clark. Philadelphia: Moore College of Art, 1984.

Kangas, Matthew. "Viola Frey's Family Plot." *Sculpture* 13 (May/June 1994): 38–43.

Viola Frey: Fresno Art Museum December 3, 1991–March 1, 1992, exh. cat. San Francisco: Rena Bransten Gallery, 1992.

KYOHEI FUJITA

Born 1921, Tokyo, Japan

p. 64

Kyohei Fujita, exh. cat. Tokyo: Asahi Shinbun, 1991.

Kyohei Fujita Museum of Glass: Selected Works. Miyagi, Japan: Kyohei Fujita Museum of Glass, Dai Nippon Printing Co., 1996.

Takeda, Atsushi. "Kyohei Fujita and His Decorative Glass Caskets." *Neues Glas* 2 (April/June 1987): 66–72.

MARY GILES

Born 1944, Saint Paul, Minnesota

p. 241

"4th Dimension: (Viewing the Impossible)." *Southwest Art* 17 (February 1988): 16.

Mary Giles/Kari Lønning, exh. cat. Wilton, Conn.: Brown/Grotta Gallery, 1995.

The 10th Wave, Part I: New Baskets and Freestanding Fiber Sculpture, exh. cat. Wilton, Conn.: Brown/Grotta Gallery, 1997.

MICHAEL GLANCY

Born 1950, Detroit, Michigan

p. 62

Constellations: An Alternative Galaxy. Glass by Michael Glancy. Text by Miklos von Bartha, Dan Klein, Dale Chihuly, and Erik Gottschalk. Basel: Edition von Bartha, 1995.

Klein, Dan. *Michael Glancy—Interaction 1991.* Basel: Edition Galerie von Bartha, 1991.

McTwigan, Michael. "Michael Glancy: Balancing Order and Chaos." *Glass* 42 (Winter 1990): 20–29.

ROBIN GREBE

Born 1957, Newark, New Jersey

p. 95

Chambers, Karen S. "Robin Grebe's Universe." *Neues Glas* 4 (1990): 294–99.

———. "Telling Tales in Glass." *Neues Glas* 3 (1994): 10–21.

Hawley, Henry H. *Glass Today: American Studio Glass from Cleveland Collections,* exh. cat. Cleveland: The Cleveland Museum of Art, 1997.

DAVID GROTH

Born 1950, Scotia, California

p. 207

Expressions in Wood: Masterworks from the Wornick Collection, exh. cat. Essays by Matthew Kangas, John Perreault, Edward S. Cooke, Jr., and Tran Turner. Oakland: Oakland Museum of California in association with University of Washington Press, Seattle, 1996.

WAYNE HIGBY

Born 1943, Colorado Springs, Colorado

pp. 170–171

Higby, Wayne. "A Search for Form and Place." *Ceramics Monthly* 37, no. 10 (December 1989): 5, 27–37.

Klemperer, Louis. "Wayne Higby." *American Ceramics* 3, no. 4 (April 1985): 32–37.

Turner, Robert. "Abstract Bowls—Emotional Connections: The Recent Work of Wayne Higby." *Ceramics: Art & Perception* 6 (1991): 25–29.

BRIAN HIRST

Born 1956, Grippsland, Victoria, Australia

p. 63

Anderson, Nola. "Object, Symbol, and Image." *Craft Arts* 9 (1987): 32–38.

Cochrane, Grace. *The Craft Movement in Australia: A History.* Kensington, NSW, Australia: University of New South Wales Press, 1992.

DAVID R. HUCHTHAUSEN

Born 1951, Wisconsin Rapids, Wisconsin

p. 61

Currents 25: David R. Huchthausen, exh. cat. Text by Sidney M. Goldstein. Saint Louis: The Saint Louis Art Museum, 1984.

Silberman, Robert. "David Huchthausen: Controlled Fragments." *American Craft* 47 (August/September 1987): 54–59.

Talaba, Mark S. "Projection and Transformation—Mysteries of the Leitungs Scherben." *Neues Glas* 3 (1983): 134–41.

ROBERT HUDSON

Born 1938, Salt Lake City, Utah

p. 180

Robert Hudson: A Survey, exh. cat. Text by Graham W. J. Beal, Jan Butterfield, and Michael Schwager. San Francisco: San Francisco Museum of Modern Art, 1985.

Robert Hudson and Richard Shaw: New Ceramic Sculpture, exh. cat. Andover, Mass.: Addison Gallery of American Art, Phillips Academy, 1998.

Robert Hudson: December 9, 1977, to January 27, 1978, exh. cat. Philadelphia: Moore College of Art Gallery, 1977.

WILLIAM HUNTER

Born 1947, Long Beach, California

p. 204

Expressions in Wood: Masterworks from the Wornick Collection, exh. cat. Essays by Matthew Kangas, John Perreault, Edward S. Cooke, Jr., and Tran Turner. Oakland: Oakland Museum of California in association with University of Washington Press, Seattle, 1996.

Hunter & Hunter: Turned and Carved Wood by William Hunter, Enamel Jewelry by Marianne Hunter, exh. cat. Los Angeles: Del Mano Gallery, 1998.

DIANE ITTER

Born 1946, Summit, New Jersey; died 1989

pp. 232–233

Diane Itter: A Retrospective, exh. cat. Curated by Ursula Ilse-Neuman. New York: American Craft Museum, 1995.

Janeiro, Jan. "Diane Itter: Textiles about Textiles." *Shuttle, Spindle & Dyepot* 26 (Summer 1995): 35–37.

McCann, Kathleen. "Diane Itter: Paying Tribute to the Artists." *Fiberarts* 19 (September/October 1992): 43–47.

KIYOMI IWATA

Born 1941, Kobe, Japan

p. 237

Hawkins, John. "Making Materials Do the Unexpected." *Fiberarts* 23 (September/October 1996): 58.

"Kiyomi Iwata/Ken Loeber." Perimeter Gallery, Chicago, exhibitions. *American Craft* 55 (April/May 1995): 82–83.

Park, Betty. "Kiyomi Iwata: A Singularity of Vision." *Fiberarts* 13 (January/February 1986): 10.

FERNE JACOBS

Born 1942, Chicago, Illinois

p. 238

Four Artists Reflect 1971–1991: Robert Ebendorf, Ferne Jacobs, Mary Ann Scherr, Joyce Scott, exh. cat. Pittsburgh: Society for Art in Crafts, 1991.

"1995 American Craft Council Awards." *American Craft* 55 (October/November 1995): 52–59.

Raithel, Janice. "Encompassing Space." *American Craft* 43, no. 2 (April/May 1983): 8–11.

GEORGES JEANCLOS

Born 1933, Paris; died 1997

p. 173

Georges Jeanclos: Terres cuites et bronzes, exh. cat. Paris-Nançay, France: Galerie Capazza, 1995.

McPherson, Anne. "Enigma with Variations: The Sculpture of Jeanclos." *American Ceramics* 10, no. 3 (Winter 1993): 42–47.

———. *The Sculpture of Georges Jeanclos*, exh. cat. Toronto: George R. Gardiner Museum of Ceramic Art, 1995.

JUN KANEKO

Born 1942, Nagoya, Japan

p. 144

Jun Kaneko: Dutch Series—Between Light and Shadow. 's Hertogenbosch, Netherlands: European Ceramic Work Centre, 1996.

Jun Kaneko: Solo Exhibition and Installation, exh. cat. Scottsdale, Ariz.: Bentley Gallery, 1994.

Kaneko, Jun. "On Being an Artist." *Ceramics Monthly* 36 (June/August 1988): 51–58.

KAREN KARNES

Born 1925, New York, New York

p. 161

Clark, Garth. *American Ceramics: 1876 to the Present.* New York: Abbeville Press, 1987.

Davis, Don. *Wheel-Thrown Ceramics.* Asheville, N.C.: Lark Books, 1998.

"Vermont Potters." *Studio Potter* 18 (December 1989): 53–67.

Koplos, Janet. "Karen Karnes." *American Ceramics* 10, no. 2 (1992): 49.

JOEY KIRKPATRICK

Born 1952, Des Moines, Iowa

pp. 114–115

Chambers, Karen. "Dual Action Artistry." *American Style* (Summer 1998): 62–69.

Hollister, Paul. "Personification of Feelings: The Mace/Kirkpatrick Collaboration." *Neues Glas* 1 (1984): 14–19.

Kirkpatrick/Mace: April 15–August 15, 1993, exh. brochure. Ames: Brunnier Gallery and Museum, Iowa State University, 1993.

JON KUHN

Born 1949, Chicago, Illinois

p. 58

Byrd, Joan Falconer. "Jon Kuhn: Radiant Vision." *American Craft* 55 (October/November 1995): 70–73.

Jon Kuhn, exh. cat. Boca Raton, Fla.: Habatat Galleries, 1997.

Jon Kuhn: Essence of Matter, exh. cat. Chicago: Marx Saunders Gallery, Ltd., 1997.

DAN KVITKA

Born 1958, Portland, Oregon

p. 205

Expressions in Wood: Masterworks from the Wornick Collection, exh. cat. Essays by Matthew Kangas, John Perreault, Edward S. Cooke, Jr., and Tran Turner. Oakland: Oakland Museum of California in association with University of Washington Press, Seattle, 1996.

Skilled Work: Craft in the Renwick Gallery, National Museum of American Art, Smithsonian Institution. Washington, D.C.: Smithsonian Institution Press, 1998.

DOMINICK LABINO

Born 1910, Clarion County, Pennsylvania; died 1987

p. 44

Dominick Labino: A Decade of Glass Craftsmanship, 1964–1974. Toledo, Ohio: Toledo Museum of Art, 1974.

Dominick Labino: Glass Retrospective. Text by Joan Falconer Byrd. Cullowhee, N.C.: Western Carolina University, 1982.

Reed, Harry. "Dominick Labino." *American Art Glass Quarterly* (Fall 1983): 60–67.

PATTI LECHMAN

Born 1946, Fort Bragg, North Carolina

p. 239

Fiber R/Evolution, exh. cat. John Porter Retzer and Florence Horn Retzer, eds., curated by Jane Brite. Milwaukee, Wis.: Milwaukee Art Museum, 1986.

Small Works in Fiber: The Mildred Constantine Collection, exh. cat. Cleveland, Ohio: Cleveland Museum of Art, 1993.

"Southern Arts Federation/National Endowment for the Arts: 1993 Crafts Fellowship." *American Craft* 54 (February/March 1994): supp. 1–12.

STANISLAV LIBENSKÝ

Stanislav Libenský, born 1921, Sezemice, Czechoslovakia

pp. 100–102

Museum Bellerive, Zurich. *Skulpturen aus Glas: Stanislav Libenský und Jaroslava Brychtová, Prag Eine Retrospektive 1945–1990.* Text by Sigrid Barten, Ludmila Vachtová, Sylva Petrová, Jaroslava Brychtová, and Stanislav Libenský. Zurich, 1990.

Stanislav Libenský/Jaroslava Brychtová: A 40-year Collaboration in Glass, exh. cat. Edited by Susanne K. Frantz with contributions by Thomas S. Buechner, Susanne K. Frantz, Sylva Petrová, and Jiří Setlik. Corning, N.Y.: The Corning Museum of Glass; Munich: Prestel, 1994.

Vašíček, Aleš. "An Interview with Stanlislav Libenský and Jaroslava Brychtová." *Glasswork* 10 (October 1991): 10–19.

MARK LINDQUIST

Born 1949, Oakland, California

pp. 210–211

Hobbs, Robert. *Mark Lindquist: Revolutions in Wood,* exh. cat. Richmond, Va.: Hand Workshop Art Center in association with University of Washington Press, Seattle, 1995.

Palladino-Craig, Allys. "Mark Lindquist: Making Split Decisions." *Art Today* (Spring 1989): 24–28, 48.

Wright, Nancy. "Mark Lindquist: The Bowl Is a Performance." *American Craft* 40, no. 5 (October/November 1980): 22–27.

MELVIN LINDQUIST

Born 1911, Kingsburg, California

pp. 212–213

Jacobson, Edward. *The Art of Turned-Wood Bowls.* Essays by Llloyd Herman, Dale L. Nish, and Rudy H. Turk. New York: Dutton, 1985.

Monroe, Michael W. *The White House Collection of American Crafts.* Essay by Barbaralee Diamonstein, foreword by Elisabeth Broun. New York: Harry N. Abrams, Inc., 1995

MARVIN LIPOFSKY

Born 1938, Barrington, Illinois

p. 46

Porges, Maria. "Artist and Educator: Marvin Lipofsky." *Neues Glas* 4 (1991): 8–15.

Waggoner, Shawn. "The Natural Form of Glass: Marvin Lipofsky." *Glass Art* (May/June 1997): 54–59.

White, Cheryl. "Marvin Lipofsky: Roving Ambassador of Glass." *American Craft* 51 (October/November 1991): 46–51.

HARVEY K. LITTLETON

Born 1922, Corning, New York

p. 45

Byrd, Joan Falconer. *Harvey K. Littleton: A Retrospective Exhibition,* exh. cat. Atlanta: High Museum of Art, 1984.

Littleton, Fujita, exh. cat. Ebeltoft, Denmark: Glasmuseum, 1989.

Warmus, William. "Harvey Littleton: Glass Master." *Glass* 72 (Special Harvey Littleton issue) (Fall 1998): 26–35.

MICHAEL LUCERO

Born 1953, Tracy, California

pp. 164–166

Failing, Patricia. "Michael Lucero: Homage to Ancient Arts." *American Craft* 55, no. 1 (February/March 1995): 32–37.

Leach, Mark Richard, Barbara J. Bloemink, and Lucy R. Lippard. *Michael Lucero: Sculpture 1976–1995,* exh. cat. New York: Hudson Hills Press in association with The Mint Museum of Art, Charlotte, N.C., 1996.

Ratcliff, Carter. "Chimeras of Clay." *Art in America* 85 (June 1997): 92–97.

FLORA C. MACE

Born 1949, Exeter, New Hampshire

pp. 114–115

Chambers, Karen. "Dual Action Artistry." *American Style* (Summer 1998): 62–69.

Hollister, Paul. "Personification of Feelings: The Mace/Kirkpatrick Collaboration." *Neues Glas* 1 (1984): 14–19.

Kirkpatrick/Mace: April 15–August 15, 1993, exh. brochure. Ames: Brunnier Gallery and Museum, Iowa State University, 1993.

JUDY KENSLEY MCKIE

Born 1944, Boston, Massachusetts

p. 254

Busch, Akiko. "Judy McKie: Connecting to the World." *American Craft* 54 (December 1994/January 1995): 32–35.

Cooke, Edward S., Jr. *New American Furniture: The Second Generation of Studio Furnituremakers,* exh. cat. Boston: Museum of Fine Arts, 1989.

Smith, Joy Cattanach. "Judy Kensley McKie." *American Craft* 43, no. 6 (December 1983/January 1984): 2–6.

SAM MALOOF

Born 1916, Chino, California

p. 197

Maloof, Sam. *Sam Maloof, Woodworker.* Tokyo: Kodansha International; New York: Kodansha America, 1983.

Stone, Michael A. "Sam Maloof." *Contemporary American Woodworkers.* Salt Lake City, Utah: G. M. Smith, 1986.

Woodenworks: Furniture Objects by Five Contemporary Craftsmen—George Nakashima, Sam Maloof, Wharton Esherick, Arthur Espenet Carpenter, Wendell Castle, exh. cat. Washington, D.C.: Renwick Gallery of the National Collection of Fine Arts, Smithsonian Institution; Saint Paul: Minnesota Museum of Art, 1972.

RICHARD MARQUIS

Born 1945, Bumblebee, Arizona

pp. 84–85

Four Leaders in Glass: Dale Chihuly, Richard Marquis, Therman Statom and Dick Weiss, exh. cat. Los Angeles: Craft and Folk Art Museum, 1980.

Matano, Koji. "Richard Marquis." Interview by author. *Glasswork* 2 (July 1989): 20–25.

Oldknow, Tina. *Richard Marquis Objects.* Seattle: University of Washington Press, 1997.

ALPHONSE MATTIA

Born 1947, Philadelphia, Pennsylvania

p. 191

Alphonse Mattia: Bookshelves Any Size, exh. cat. New York: Peter Joseph Gallery, 1993.

Cooke, Edward S., Jr. *New American Furniture: The Second Generation of Studio Furnituremakers,* exh. cat. Boston: Museum of Fine Arts, 1989.

Jeffri, Joan, ed. *The Craftsperson Speaks: Artists in Varied Media Discuss Their Crafts.* Introduction by Mary Greeley. New York: Greenwood Press, 1992.

MARI MÉSZÁROS

Born 1949, Tiszaszentimre, Hungary

p. 111

Klotz, Uta M. "The Poetry of the Fragment: Mari Mészáros." *Neues Glas* 2 (1995): 38–45.

Mari Mészáros: Glass Sculptures, exh. cat. Eefde, Netherlands: Artterre Gallery, 1997.

Recent Glass Sculpture: A Union of Ideas, exh. cat. Curated by Audrey Mann. Milwaukee, Wis.: Milwaukee Art Museum, 1997.

KLAUS MOJE

Born 1936, Hamburg, Germany

pp. 76–79

Edwards, Geoffrey. *Klaus Moje Glass/Glas: A Retrospective Exhibition,* exh. cat. Melbourne, Australia: National Gallery of Victoria, 1995.

Klaus Moje/Dale Chihuly, exh. cat. Text by Finn Lynggaard, Helmut Ricke, and Karen S. Chambers. Ebeltoft, Denmark: Glasmuseum, 1991.

Waggoner, Shawn. "The Work of Klaus Moje: A New Order." *Glass Art* (May/June 1992): 4–8.

WILLIAM MORRIS

Born 1957, Carmel, California

pp. 86–93, front cover (detail)

Blonston, Gary. *William Morris: Artifacts/Glass.* New York: Abbeville Press, 1996.

Elliott, Kate, ed. *William Morris Glass: Artifact and Art.* Seattle: University of Washington Press, 1989.

Myth, Object, and the Animal, exh. cat. Text by James Yood. Norfolk, Va.: Chrysler Museum of Art; Billings, Mont.: Yellowstone Art Museum; Fort Wayne, Ind.: Fort Wayne Museum of Art, 1999.

EDWARD MOULTHROP

Born 1916, Rochester, New York

p. 208

Monroe, Michael W. *The White House Collection of American Crafts.* Essay by Barbaralee Diamonstein, foreword by Elisabeth Broun. New York: Harry N. Abrams, Inc., 1995.

Skilled Work: Craft in the Renwick Gallery, National Museum of American Art, Smithsonian Institution. Washington, D.C.: Smithsonian Institution Press, 1998.

Smith, Helen C. "Turning: Ed Moulthrop." *American Craft* 39, no. 6 (December 1979/January 1980): 18–23.

JAY MUSLER

Born 1949, Sacramento, California

p. 94

Hammel, Lisa. "An Apocalyptic Art." *American Craft* 48 (October/November 1988): 26–31.

Hollister, Paul. "Jay Musler's Painted Glass: The Face of Anger." *Neues Glas* 1 (January/March 1985): 12–19.

Musler, Jay. "Matter." *Glass Art Society Journal* (1994): 59–60.

JOEL PHILIP MYERS

Born 1934, Paterson, New Jersey

pp. 80–81

Boylen, Michael. "Compositions on Black: Joel Philip Myers." *American Craft* 40, no. 5 (October–November 1980): 8–11.

Hollister, Paul. "Joel Philip Myers's Glass: 'A Quiet, Peaceful Way of Working.'" *Neues Glas* 3 (1983): 128–33.

Joel Philip Myers, exh. cat. Ebeltoft, Denmark: Glasmuseum, 1993.

RON NAGLE

Born 1939, San Francisco, California

pp. 162–163

Berkson, Bill. "Nagle Wares." *American Craft* 57 (August/September 1997): 36–41.

Moser, Charlotte. "Ron Nagle: Recent Work." *Ceramics Monthly* 42 (June/August 1994): 41–47.

Ron Nagle: A Survey Exhibition 1958–1993, exh. cat. Oakland: Mills College Art Gallery, 1993.

ERIC NELSEN
Born 1954, Seattle, Washington
p. 184
Ament, Deloris Tarzan. "To Fire the Anagama . . ." *Art Access* 6 (March 1997): 5.
Josslin, Victoria. "Disorder a Reality for Two Artists." *Seattle Post-Intelligencer*, 12 February 1999.
Krafft, Charles. "Eric Nelsen at William Traver." *Reflex* 5 (May/June 1991): 25.

MANUEL NERI
Born 1930, Sanger, California
pp. 255–256
Jones, Caroline A. *Manuel Neri: Plasters.* San Francisco: San Francisco Museum of Modern Art, 1989.
Manuel Neri: Early Work, 1953–1978, exh. cat. Text by Price Amerson, John Beardsley, Jack Cowart, Henry Geldzahler, and Robert Pincus. New York: Hudson Hills Press in association with The Corcoran Gallery of Art, Washington, D.C., 1996.
Neubert, George. *Manuel Neri, Sculptor.* exh. cat. Oakland: The Oakland Museum, 1976.

BRETISLAV NOVAK, JR.
Born 1952, Semily, Czechoslovakia
p. 98
Patti, Thomas. "The Glass of Bretislav Novak Jr." *Collector Editions* (Spring 1986): 24–25.

THOMAS PATTI
Born 1943, Pittsfield, Massachusetts
pp. 48–49
Currents 24: Tom Patti, exh. cat. Text by Sidney M. Goldstein. Saint Louis: The Saint Louis Art Museum, 1984.
Hollister, Paul. "The Code Is in the Glass." *Neues Glas* 2 (April/June 1983): 74–83.
Tom Patti: Glass, exh. cat. Springfield, Mass.: The George Walter Vincent Smith Art Museum, 1980.

MARK PEISER
Born 1938, Chicago, Illinois
pp. 54–55
Byrd, Joan Falconer. "Mark Peiser." *New Work* 37 (Spring 1989): 8–14.
Hollister, Paul. "Mark Peiser: Explorations of Inner Space." *Neues Glas* 3 (July/September 1984): 126–33.
Michelson, Maureen. "Profile: Mark Peiser." *Glass* 9, no. 1 (January 1982): 74–80.

MICHAEL JAMES PETERSON
Born 1952, Wichita Falls, Texas
p. 202
Expressions in Wood: Masterworks from the Wornick Collection, exh. cat. Essays by Matthew Kangas, John Perreault, Edward S. Cooke, Jr., and Tran Turner. Oakland: Oakland Museum of California in association with University of Washington Press, Seattle, 1996.

KEN PRICE
Born 1935, Los Angeles, California
pp. 158–160
Ceramic Sculpture: Six Artists, exh. cat. Text by Suzanne Foley and Richard Marshall. New York, Seattle, and London: Whitney Museum of American Art, New York, 1981.
Lebow, Edward. "Ken Price." *American Ceramics* 7, no. 2 (1989): 16–25.
Simon, Joan. "An Interview with Ken Price." *Art in America* 68, no. 1 (January 1980): 98–104.

NARCISSUS QUAGLIATA
Born 1942, Rome, Italy
p. 41
Blalock, Dolores. "Narcissus Quagliata." *American Art Glass Quarterly* (Fall 1983): 36–57.
Narcissus Quagliata: Painting with Light / pitture di luce / pintando con luz, exh. cat. Essays by Kenneth R. Trapp and Rosa Barovier Mentasti. Rome: Il Cigno Galileo Galilei, 1996.
Quagliata, Narcissus. *Stained Glass from Mind to Light: An Inquiry into the Nature of the Medium.* San Francisco: Mattole Press, 1976.

CLIFFORD RAINEY
Born 1948, Whitehead, County Antrim, Northern Ireland
pp. 125–127
Clifford Rainey. Sculpture & Drawings 1967–1987, exh. cat. Text by Liam Kelly. Belfast: Arts Council of Northern Ireland; Dublin: Douglas Hyde Gallery, 1987.
Kelly, Liam. "Clifford Rainey." *Glass Art Society Journal* (1987): 58–60.
Porges, Maria. "Clifford Rainey." *Sculpture* 17, no. 3 (March 1998): 59–60.

DAVID REGAN
Born 1964, Buffalo, New York
p. 169
Adlin, Jane. *Contemporary Ceramics: Selections from The Metropolitan Museum of Art.* New York: The Metropolitan Museum of Art, 1998.
Davis, Don. *Wheel-Thrown Ceramics.* Asheville, N.C.: Lark Books, 1998.
Knight, Christopher. "David Regan." *Art Issues* (January/February 1997): 46.

DANIEL RHODES
Born 1911, Fort Dodge, Iowa; died 1989
pp. 134–135
Daniel Rhodes: The California Years, exh. cat. Text by Gary Smith. Santa Cruz, Calif.: The Art Museum of Santa Cruz County, 1986.

McDonald, Robert. "Daniel Rhodes." *American Craft* 46 (February/March 1986): 18–21.

Rhodes, Daniel. "The Search for Form." *Studio Potter* 13 (December 1984): 1–20.

TOM RIPPON

Born 1954, Sacramento, California

p. 172

Clark, Garth. *American Ceramics: 1876 to the Present.* New York: Abbeville Press, 1987.

Tom Rippon: A Poet's Game, exh. cat. Text by Nancy Bless. Sheboygan, Mich.: John Michael Kohler Art Center, 1993.

ED ROSSBACH

Born 1914, Chicago, Illinois

p. 236

Ed Rossbach: 40 Years of Exploration and Innovation in Fiber Art, exh. cat. Asheville, N.C.: Lark Books in association with Textile Museum, Washington, D.C., 1990.

Janeiro, Jan. "Ed Rossbach: Prizing the Journey." *American Craft* 50 (June/July 1990): 40–45.

Ties That Bind: Fiber Art by Ed Rossbach and Katherine Westphal from the Daphne Farago Collection, exh. cat. Essays by Paul J. Smith and Jan Janeiro. Providence: Providence Museum of Art and Rhode Island School of Design, 1997.

JERRY ROTHMAN

Born 1933, Brooklyn, New York

p. 145

Entous, Karen Alpert. "Visiting Jerry Rothman." *Ceramics Monthly* 33 (February 1985): 53.

Folk, Thomas C. "Jerry Rothman: Studio Potter and Sculptor." *Ceramics: Art & Perception* 5 (1991): 36–41.

Levin, Elaine. "Jerry Rothman: A *Ceramics Monthly* Portfolio." *Ceramics Monthly* 40 (November 1992): 55–60.

GINNY RUFFNER

Born 1952, Atlanta, Georgia

p. 83

Kangas, Matthew. "Unraveling Ruffner." *Glass* 43 (Spring 1991): 20–29.

Miller, Bonnie M. *Why Not? The Art of Ginny Ruffner,* exh. cat. Introduction by Arthur C. Danto. Tacoma, Wash.: Tacoma Art Museum in association with University of Washington Press, Seattle and London, 1995.

Waggoner, Shawn. "With Visibility Comes Greater Responsibility: A Conversation with Ginny Ruffner." *Glass Art* 7, no. 2 (January/February 1992): 4–8.

JANE SAUER

Born 1937, Saint Louis, Missouri

p. 240

Degener, Patricia. "Emotive Basketry." *American Craft* 46, no. 4 (August/September 1986): 42–47, 59.

Falconer, Crisa Meahl. "The Knotted Sculpture of Jane Sauer." *Fiberarts* 13 (May/June 1986): 31–33.

Van Deventer, M. J. "Jane Sauer." *Art Gallery International* (May/June 1989): 42–45.

ADRIAN SAXE

Born 1943, Glendale, California

pp. 146–147

Adrian Saxe, exh. cat. Kansas City: University of Missouri, Kansas City Gallery of Art, 1987.

Clark, Garth. "Adrian Saxe: An Interview." *American Ceramics* 1, no. 4 (1982): 23–29.

Lynn, Martha Drexler. *The Clay Art of Adrian Saxe,* exh. cat. Los Angeles: Los Angeles County Museum of Art; New York: Thames and Hudson, 1993.

ITALO SCANGA

Born 1932, Lago, Calabria, Italy

p. 129

Angels and Saints: Dale Chihuly and Italo Scanga, exh. cat. Aspen, Colo.: Susan Duval Gallery, 1994.

Italo Scanga. Seattle: Portland Press, 1993.

Tomisy, Paul. *Italo Scanga 1972–1985,* exh. cat. Oakland: The Oakland Museum Art Department, 1986.

CYNTHIA SCHIRA

Born 1934, Pittsfield, Massachusetts

p. 225

Corwin, Nancy A. "Cynthia Schira: Image in Structure." *Surface Design Journal* 14, no. 1 (Fall 1989): 4–8.

Cynthia Schira: New Work, exh. cat. Exhibition organized by Laura M. Giles, text by Nancy Corwin. Lawrence: Spencer Museum of Art, University of Kansas, 1984.

Park, Betty. "Poetic Evocations: The Woven Cloth of Cynthia Schira." *American Craft* 5, no. 5 (October/November 1985): 18–22.

JUNE SCHWARCZ

Born 1918, Denver, Colorado

p. 252

Bennett, Jamie. "June Schwarcz: A Conversation with Jamie Bennett." *Metalsmith* 3, no. 3 (Summer 1983): 30–35.

June Schwarcz: Forty Years/Forty Pieces, exh. cat. Curated by Carole Austin. San Francisco: San Francisco Craft and Folk Art Museum, 1998.

Lynn, Vanessa S. "June Schwarcz: The Malleable Vessel." *Metalsmith* 10 (Summer 1990): 20–23.

KAY SEKIMACHI

Born 1926, San Francisco, California

pp. 244–247, title page

Alba, Victoria. "Against the Grain: Consuelo Jimenez Underwood and Kay Sekimachi." *Fiberarts* 20, no. 2 (September/October 1993): 35–41.

Mayfield, Signe. *Marriage in Form: Kay Sekimachi and Bob Stocksdale.* Palo Alto, Calif.: Palo Alto Cultural Center, 1993.

Mayfield, Signe. "Profile of an Artist: Kay Sekimachi." *Shuttle, Spindle & Dyepot* 25, no. 1 (Winter 1993/94): 33–35.

RICHARD SHAW

Born 1941, Hollywood, California

pp. 176–177

Ceramic Sculpture: Six Artists, exh. cat. Text by Suzanne Foley and Richard Marshall. New York, Seattle, and London: Whitney Museum of American Art, New York, 1981.

Richard Shaw. Illusionism in Clay: 1971–1985, exh. cat. San Francisco: Braunstein Gallery, 1985.

White, Cheryl. "Master of Illusion Richard Shaw." *American Ceramics* 6, no. 2 (1987): 30–37.

MICHAEL SHULER

Born 1950, Trenton, New Jersey

pp. 214–215

Expressions in Wood: Masterworks from the Wornick Collection, exh. cat. Essays by Matthew Kangas, John Perreault, Edward S. Cooke, Jr., and Tran Turner. Oakland: Oakland Museum of California in association with University of Washington Press, Seattle, 1996.

Monroe, Michael W. *The White House Collection of American Crafts.* Essay by Barbaralee Diamonstein, foreword by Elizabeth Broun. New York: Harry N. Abrams, Inc., 1995.

KARYL SISSON

Born 1948, Brooklyn, New York

p. 235

Colchester, Chloe. *The New Textile: Trends and Traditions.* New York: Rizzoli, 1991.

Jane Sauer/Karyl Sisson, exh. cat. Wilton, Conn.: Brown/Grotta Gallery, 1995.

Muchnic, Suzanne. "Karyl Sisson: The Ordinary Transformed." *American Craft* 55, no. 6 (December 1995/January 1996): 46–49.

KIKI SMITH

Born 1954, Nuremberg, Germany

p. 230, spine (detail)

Kiki Smith, exh. cat. Texts by Paolo Columbo, Elizabeth Janus, Eduardo Lipshutz-Villa, Robin Winters, and Kiki Smith. The Hague: ICA; Amsterdam: Sdu Publishers, 1990.

Posner, Helaine. *Kiki Smith.* Boston: Bulfinch, 1998.

Shearer, Linda, and Claudia Gould. *Kiki Smith,* exh. cat. Text by Marguerite Yourcenar. Williamstown, Mass.: Williams College Museum of Art; Columbus: Wexner Center for the Arts, The Ohio State University, 1992.

PAUL SOLDNER

Born 1921, Summerfield, Illinois

pp. 132–133, back cover

Paul Soldner: A Retrospective, exh. cat. Organized and with text by Mary Davis MacNaughton, Elaine Levin, and Mac McLain. Claremont, Calif.: Lang Gallery, Scripps College, in association with University of Washington Press, Seattle and London, 1991.

Roberts, David. "Magic Potter." *Ceramic Review* 109 (January/February 1988): 34–38.

Williams, Gerry. "Romancing the Clay." *Studio Potter* 23 (June 1995): 48–70.

ROBERT SPERRY

Born 1927, Bushnell, Illinois

p. 142

Robert Sperry: A Retrospective, exh. cat. Preface by Jeffrey Moore, text by LaMar Harrington and Matthew Kangas. Bellevue, Wash.: Bellevue Art Museum, 1985.

Sperry, Robert. "Portfolio: Abstractions in Black and White." *Ceramics Monthly* 38 (June/August 1990): 33–40.

RUDOLF STAFFEL

Born 1911, San Antonio, Texas

p. 154

Koplos, Janet. "Rudolf Staffel: Playful Magician of Light." *American Ceramics* 9 (Summer 1991): 18–25.

Rudolf Staffel: Searching for Light, exh. cat. Essay by Marianne Aav. Helsinki, Finland: Museum of Applied Arts, 1996.

Transparency in Clay: Rudy Staffel, exh. cat. Foreword by Yvonne G.J.M. Joris, text by Ivy L. Barsky and Stephen Berg. 's Hertogenbosch, Netherlands: Museum Voor Hedendaagse Kunst Het Kruithuis, 1990.

JAY STANGER

Born 1956, Boston, Massachusetts

p. 196

"Portfolio." *American Craft* 51 (February/March 1991): 50–59.

THERMAN STATOM

Born 1953, Winterhaven, Florida

p. 82

Chambers, Karen S. "Therman Statom: On the Brink." *Neues Glas* 4 (1994): 8–19.

Four Leaders in Glass: Dale Chihuly, Richard Marquis, Therman Statom and Dick Weiss, exh. cat. Los Angeles: Craft and Folk Art Museum, 1980.

Nzegwu, Nkiru. "Living in a Glass House, Passing through Glass: The Art of Therman Statom, James Watkins, and John Dowell, Jr." *International Review of African American Art* 11, no. 2 (1994): 44–51.

BOB STOCKSDALE

Born 1913, Warren, Indiana

pp. 216–219

Duncan, Robert Bruce. "Bob Stocksdale: Still on a Roll at 75." *Woodwork* 1 (Spring 1989): 16–21.

La Trobe-Bateman, Richard. "World-Class Turner." *American Craft* 47, no. 6 (December 1987/January 1988): 30–35.

Mayfield, Signe. *Marriage in Form: Kay Sekimachi and Bob Stocksdale.* Palo Alto, Calif.: Palo Alto Cultural Center, 1993.

LINO TAGLIAPIETRA

Born 1934, Murano, Italy

p. 47

Barovier, Marino, ed. *Tagliapietra: A Venetian Glass Maestro.* Dublin: Links for Publishing Ltd., 1998.

Lino Tagliapietra: 18th May–6th October 1996, exh. cat. Ebeltoft, Denmark: Glasmuseum, 1996.

Marquis, Richard. "Maestro Lino." *American Craft* 57 (December 1997/January 1998): 40–45.

IRVIN TEPPER

Born 1947, Saint Louis, Missouri

p. 155

Clark, Garth. *American Ceramics: 1876 to the Present.* New York: Abbeville Press, 1987.

Irvin Tepper: Cups, Drawings, Stories, exh. cat. Newport Beach, Calif.: Newport Harbor Art Museum, 1983.

Schimmel, Paul. "Conversation Pieces: The Cups of Irvin Tepper." *American Ceramics* 3, no. 2 (1984): 30–39.

KARLA TRINKLEY

Born 1956, Yardley, Pennsylvania

pp. 96–97

Hawly, Henry H. *Glass Today: American Studio Glass from the Cleveland Collections*, exh. cat. Cleveland: Cleveland Museum of Art, 1997.

Lynn, Martha Dexter. *Masters of Contemporary Glass: Selections from the Glick Collection*, exh. cat. Contributions by Barry Shifman. Indianapolis: Indianapolis Museum of Art in cooperation with Indiana University Press, Bloomington, 1997.

Miller, Bonnie J. "Karla Trinkley: Silent Spaces." *New Work* 31 (Fall 1987): 24–25.

ROBERT TURNER

Born 1913, Port Washington, New York

pp. 140–141

Doubet, Ward. "Robert Turner." *American Ceramics* 9, no. 4 (1991): 18–25.

Hays, Johanna Burstein. "Robert Turner." *American Ceramics* 3, no. 4 (1985): 50–57.

Robert Turner: A Potter's Retrospective, exh. cat. Milwaukee, Wis.: Milwaukee Art Museum, 1985.

DE WAIN VALENTINE

Born 1936, Fort Collins, Colorado

p. 51

De Wain Valentine: New Work, exh. cat. Los Angeles: Los Angeles County Museum of Art, 1979.

Ellis, George, Liala Twigg-Smith, and Melinda Wortz. *De Wain Valentine Recent Works.* Honolulu: Contemporary Art Center and Honolulu Academy of Arts, 1985.

BERTIL VALLIEN

Born 1938, Stockholm, Sweden

pp. 118–124

Bertil Vallien, exh. cat. Text by Gunnar Lindqvist. Ebeltoft, Denmark: Glasmuseum, 1994.

Lindqvist, Gunnar. *Bertil Vallien.* Translated by Angela Adegren. Stockholm: Carlsson Bokförlag, 1990.

Lindqvist, Gunnar. "Bertil Vallien: Glass Art Innovator, Metaphysical Explorer." *Neues Glas* 2 (1996): 18–25.

FRANTISEK VÍZNER

Born 1936, Prague, Czechoslovakia

pp. 52–53

Vízner, Frantisek. "Frantisek Vízner." *Glass Art Society Journal* (1989): 23–26.

Vízner, Frantisek. "1984 G.A.S. Conference Featured Artists: Frantisek Vízner." *Glass Art Society Journal* (1984–85): 94–95.

Warmus, William. "Frantisek Vízner." *New Work* 33 (Spring 1988): 26–27.

PETER VOULKOS

Born 1924, Bozeman, Montana

pp. 136–139

Peter Voulkos Retrospective, exh. cat. Tokyo: Sezon Bijutsukan, 1995.

Slivka, Rose. *Peter Voulkos: A Dialogue with Clay.* New York: New York Graphic Society in association with American Crafts Council, New York, 1978.

Slivka, Rose, and Karen Tsujimoto. *The Art of Peter Voulkos*, exh. cat. Tokyo: Kodansha International in collaboration with The Oakland Museum, 1995.

JANUSZ WALENTYNOWICZ

Born 1956, Dygowo, Poland

p. 109

Hawley, Henry H. *Glass Today: American Studio Glass from Cleveland Collections*, exh. cat. Cleveland: The Cleveland Museum of Art, 1997.

Netzer, Sylvia. "Janusz A. Walentynowicz." *Neues Glas* 4 (1993): 8–17.

"Portfolio." *American Craft* 51 (August/September 1991): 48–51.

HANS JOACHIM WEISSFLOG

Born 1954, Hönnersum, Germany

p. 221

Nicola, Karl-Günter. "Drechseln in den Sternen: Hans Joachim Weissflog." *Kunsthandwerk & Design* 2 (1996): 28–31.

Nolte, Martin. "Hans Joachim Weissflog." *Woodturning* 6 (January/February 1992): 45–48.

"Weissflog Receives German Craft Award." *Turning Points* 6, no. 3 (Fall 1993/Winter 1994): 5.